BOLD

ON THE

INSIDE

Amplify Your Impact
Without Raising Your Voice

Trailblazer Publishing

Phoenix, Arizona

www.nicolelance.co

TRAILBLAZER
PUBLISHING

Cover Design & Art: Chani Becker (ChaniBecker.com)

Publishing Alchemist: Heather N. Wilde (HezzieMae.com)

ISBN: 979-8-9871006-7-7

BOLD ON THE INSIDE

Amplify Your Impact
Without Raising Your Voice

Nicole Lance

www.nicolelance.co

Other books by Nicole Lance

Awesome On Your Own Terms: *Intentional Practices to Help You Stop Shoulding and Start Succeeding*

Hot Tub Mommy: *Do All Moms Swear This Much?*

Bold on the Inside: *Amplify Your Impact Without Raising Your Voice*

Dedication:

To my mom, Sherry Dailey, and to Kathi Warner, Joyce Hollis, Lynne Jeffrey, and Diane Cichinsky for also "momming" me over the years. You are a bold bunch of women, and I am who I am because of you.

And to Emersyn - may you always be as bold on the inside as your clothing choices are on the outside. Go get 'em, baby girl.

Table of Contents

Unicorn Poop
and Other Important Questions

What color is a unicorn? What color is a unicorn's mane? Is its horn straight or twisted? Can it fly? Most importantly, my daughter's book says unicorns poop tiny puffs of cotton candy—is this true?

Before you put this book down, shaking your head and wondering, "What the heck is this?" hang in there with me. Go back and answer those questions. I bet something like white, pink, or rainbow popped into your head first. But what about silver? Or sparkly purple? Incandescent turquoise? Why couldn't their horns be twisted, straight, or even both? Maybe they don't have wings (because, as any other My Little Pony aficionado knows, that would make it an alicorn), but they're magical beings, and it wouldn't surprise me one bit if they could fly. And of all the things I've ever hoped for, I absolutely hope it's true that unicorns do poop tiny puffs of cotton candy.

Unless you've had a completely different life experience than I have—in which case we are DEFINITELY meeting for coffee—you've probably never seen an actual unicorn. Consequently, neither of us actually knows what one might look like, let alone what many unicorns look like. Moral of the story?

There's no one right way to be a unicorn.

Same, too, with leadership. There are a million models on leadership, some good, some not so good, and a million different types of leaders. There are plenty of fictionalized ideals and false stories floating around out there trying to get you to show up in a specific way. How many of these do you even resonate with? Maybe you've been told you're too quiet, too direct, too friendly, too disorganized, too social, too Type B. It's also very possible you've been told you're too loud, too empathetic, too abrasive, too controlling, too reserved, too Type A. I bet you, just like I do, look at these leaders and models and don't see yourself. Where are the ones who are leading the way you want to lead?

Now think about leaders you have resonated with. Think of the people you've seen in action who have been incredible at guiding others and getting a whole lot accomplished. Consider how different each of them are. I'm betting that most of them look very different than these other more popularized models of leadership. Unless you've had a completely different life experience than I have—and in which case, again, we are DEFINITELY meeting for coffee—all of these people lead uniquely with their own distinct energy and approach. Moral of the story?

There's no one right way to be a leader.

In my decades of leadership coaching, I've found the common thread among the most successful leaders isn't anything they do externally. They don't speak in similar manners, lead meetings or 1:1 discussions in the same way, or even embody the same type of executive presence. They do all have a similar internal orientation, however: *They're bold on the inside*.

Throughout the span of my career in the non-profit, local government, and private industries, I have eagerly studied leaders in action to discover what works and what doesn't. I've always been drawn to leaders who weren't afraid to make courageous choices or to do something outside the norms of expectation. Some of my most formative career experiences came from observing leaders standing up for people who were being mistreated and making courageous decisions for the right reasons, regardless of the outcome for themselves.

I especially resonated with women and queer leaders who relentlessly carved their own paths despite obstacles that would have dissuaded many others. As I developed my own leadership approach, I was consistently described as fearless but rarely felt that way on the inside. It took a lot of experimenting to identify internal practices to help me stay bold regardless of what challenge I faced. Over time, I learned to stand more firmly in my integrity and to rely on my instincts and intuition rather than letting someone else tell me how I should be showing up.

I witnessed women making stands against workplace harassment and bullying. I watched queer leaders brave new and potentially unfriendly environments and address misgendering in front of large audiences. I've watched extremely seasoned leaders be willing to make significant changes to longstanding practices, and I've seen up-and-coming leaders respectfully and effectively challenge outdated workplace practices. Each leader I observed did things in their own way, but they were all equally bold on the inside.

This book maps out 16 tactics I've discovered through my executive coaching and leadership consulting practice, as well as my own experience that serve as key strategies for leaders who want to embrace their unique leadership identity. Each chapter includes an explanation of the strategy, an illustrative story about how I've used it in action in real life, practices for how you can learn to leverage it, and integration questions to help you incorporate your understanding of each strategy into changed behaviors and practices of your own.

The world needs you out there leading exactly the way that's best for you so your impact is amplified. Whether you want to poop tiny puffs of cotton candy or simply want to be a great leader (or both!), these strategies will help you become bold on the inside so you can lead the way you want to. Let's do this!

Strategy #1:

Own Your Energy

The only person who should be in charge of your energy is YOU. This is often easier said than done, but it's a critical step—maybe the most important of them all—in truly being bold on the inside.

Think of this practice as setting your own tone for your time rather than letting other people or outside situations influence how you feel. Not only do you have an impenetrable force field around you to keep your positive energy in and keep negative energy out, but you consciously shift your energy as needed. You're conscious of how people and situations feel when approaching them, and you're cognizant of maintaining your desired emotional state while interacting with them. It's not that you don't ever feel upset or experience negativity, frustration, or anger. It's that when you do experience those things—and you will—you're able to choose how you'd like to feel instead of letting that person, situation, or feeling run away with you.

In Action: Own Your Energy

I occasionally struggle with insomnia. It gets markedly worse if I'm not managing my energy correctly, and the other morning, I was awake from about 1:15 to 2:15 a.m., then woke up again at about 4:45 a.m. with zero hope of going back to sleep. I felt discouraged for the day and frustrated with the bad night of sleep. Taking my own advice, I decided to get up, take a few deep breaths, and get my meditation space ready. There's not much to this area besides my big yellow chair, a fuzzy blanket my puppy constantly tries to steal, and a side table with a few candles on it, so in no time, I was sinking down, eyes closed, taking a few deep breaths. I started off with a simple emphasis on gratitude, calling to mind all the things I was grateful for. Of course, there's always so much when you start to focus on it! I could feel my mood begin to lift, and a small smile threatened to disrupt the scowl on my face.

After a few minutes of focusing on gratitude, I started to envision the kind of day I wanted to have instead of the one I felt was in store based on my lack of sleep and how my energy felt when I woke up. I pictured myself relaxed, happy, and productive rather than anxious, tense, and tired. I imagined some of the things I would accomplish without worrying about a massive to-do list. As I lightened up, I even explored the question, "What would make today feel good?"

Ahhh... Energy shifted. I was still physically tired but felt much more ready to start the day. Then, my daughter woke up 30 minutes earlier than usual and let the puppy out of the crate. I lovingly refer to this duo as Chaos (my daughter) and Cleo (the puppy) for good reason. As soon as the two of them connect, there's no telling what we're in for.

Cleo started by dragging out every available child's toy that had been left within snatching distance and flagrantly disrespecting my daughter by chewing each one in succession while making full eye contact. My daughter added her own flair to the experience by yelling and shouting at her maximum decibel level for the entirety of the interaction. That was followed by my daughter's usual morning rebellion of open defiance of toothbrushing and a molecular-level meltdown because the outfit she wanted to wear to school was dirty and required a change. Standing in the kitchen with a now-lukewarm cup of coffee, I wondered what the heck happened to my energy.

Time to shift it again. There wasn't time for silent reflection and meditation, but I needed to boost my levels so I could show up for my kid like the parent I wanted to be. I was determined to reclaim my day. One Taylor Swift song, some barking (from the dog, not me this time), and some booty-shaking later, and I was good to go. School drop-off went smoothly, and I came home to a blessedly quiet house and was able to get to work. It's not always easy to own your energy, but it is always important to do so.

Practices to Help You Own Your Energy

1. Recognize where you're at.

It never ceases to amaze me how many leaders walk around completely unaware of how they're actually doing and feeling. Heck, I did the same thing for a long time! It's tempting to dive right into the to-do list, jump right into the conversation, or hit the ground running the second you get into the office or get your work day started. However, I believe self-awareness is the most fundamental beginning point for excellent leadership, and you need to take at least a little bit of time to read your own pulse before you get started on anything.

This isn't just a "one and done in the morning" kind of thing, either. In practice, this is multiple check-ins throughout the day, particularly when you're switching gears or engaging in new or different interactions. When I talk about checking in to recognize where you're at, I don't mean you need two weeks in a yurt in the middle of a forest somewhere. This is a quick pause to look inward and assess yourself on a scale that makes sense to you.

There's a meme I love and often think of when I'm doing my own personal check-in. It's a giant floating rubber duck that's slowly deflating over nine separate pictures. It starts off fully inflated in the first picture, but by the last picture, it's epically deflated and sagging completely into the water. Across the top, it says, "On a 1-9 rubber duck scale, how are things going lately?"

Sometimes, I'm clearly a one and feel fully inflated, but often, I'll find myself more in the middle of the scale or occasionally feeling like I'm face down in the water. Regardless of where I'm landing, it's critical information to know so I can resource myself accordingly. I might even rearrange my schedule or postpone meetings if my energy isn't right for that type of activity. As I boost my awareness to know my starting point better, I can act more intentionally. To quote G.I. Joe, "Now you know, and knowing is half the battle."

2. Know your energy sources.

You've got to know your energy sources. What are the practices, people, places, or food sources that genuinely re-energize you and help you shift your mood and find a good feeling again? This strategy can take a bit of detective work on your part to figure out. I assumed this was a no-brainer when I started working with this tactic, but I actually had quite a bit to learn. Sure, I loved snagging an iced macchiato in the afternoon to perk me back up, and I had a couple of text threads going with friends that I would drop in on throughout the day to vent or share snarky memes with. However, as I started paying attention to what provided energy back to me, I gained some critical insights.

First, I wasn't sleeping enough. It didn't matter how much meditation I did or how many lattes I downed; that was a deficit I needed to pay attention to, and it required some lifestyle changes to make it happen. Second, I needed to be more strategic in my breakfast and lunch selections in order to feel better throughout the afternoon. Grabbing whatever was available or using my busyness as an excuse to eat something that wasn't truthfully going to fuel me wasn't going to cut it anymore if I wanted to be energized. Third, while those text threads provided a few snorts and the occasional real-life LOL, the tone of the conversations tended to be negative rather than uplifting. I didn't need to ditch my friends, but I needed to change how we communicated and connected.

I've also discovered my work environment highly impacts my energy. I spent a lot of years (decades!) working in messy spaces, justifying each one by my busyness. Who has time to get those things filed and put away neatly? Have you seen my schedule?! However, if I genuinely want to have the best energy in my workspace as possible, I need:

- An uncluttered, organized workspace with little to no external storage or piles
- Subtle tones with pops of color in strategic places; I used to decorate in lots of bright colors with photos everywhere and plants in colorful pots, but now it feels overwhelming if it's too busy visually
- Decorations that I've intentionally chosen to bring into the space as opposed to lots of little tchotchkes or items that are there just because someone gave them to me

Knowing the who, what, and how of helpful energy sources can massively impact how you show up for yourself and others. These are simple shifts with high impact that only require cultivating a bit more self-awareness.

3. Fund your energy.

Funding your energy means focusing on your inputs so you have energy for the outputs you want. What are you investing in, or how are you investing in yourself, so you have the energetic availability to do what you want to do? It's one thing to know your energy sources and an entirely different thing to fund your energy. I'm a big fan of the saying, "Hope is not a method." I am not going to hope my way into having healthy savings accounts or ample financial investments. I will have to fund these if I want them to be present.

Same goes with energy. I'm not going to wake up in the

morning or hit a lull in the afternoon and simply hope I can muster the energy to get through my day. I need to intentionally fund my energy if I rely on it as a power source. So, too, for you. You've got to put in the time and create the space for things that fund your energy. Hope can't be your method.

4. Shield and shift your energy.

In the 1989 Batman movie with Michael Keaton (also known in our household as "The Best Batman"), there's a scene in which Batman and Vicki Vale escape from the Joker's henchmen. They jump out of the Batmobile, and as they're running away, Batman utters the word "shields," and the Batmobile instantly activates an impenetrable set of shields that securely covers the entirety of the vehicle. This is how I want you to think of shielding your energy.

If you've ever walked past a couple arguing in the grocery store or sat near someone having a tense or even explosive conversation with someone else during a meeting, you can feel that difficult energy. The same thing happens when you come home from work, and although you've had a great day, someone else in your household hasn't, and their grumpiness or pain starts to infiltrate your energy. In those instances, I want you to pull out your gruffest Batman voice and say to yourself, "Shields!" and imagine you're instantly protected from that energy. You can still interact with the person or exist in the same space if you need to, but you don't have to internalize their energy.

Another way of thinking about this is to pay close

attention to whose voice is in your head and how loud or important you're allowing it to be. I had a conversation with a friend the other day about a significant shift she was about to make, and she shared a concern about what a particular person in her industry would say about it. Knowing the person in question, I didn't disagree with her. He probably would say something unkind about it.

As we explored it, though, I reminded her that just because someone else's voice is inside your head doesn't mean you have to listen to it. Not everyone gets a seat at your personal table of mentor masterminds. Be your own bouncer and kick those voices right back out onto the other side of your shield. They can knock at your door, but you don't have to let them back in.

If preventative measures haven't worked or you just plain have something crummy happen, you've got to get your shift together. Remember all those energy sources you identified? Put them to work! I always find it best to have ones that fall into major energy shift categories for me and some that are minor. Sometimes, I need a two-hour massage or a sweaty workout at the gym, and other times, I need to curl up with my puppy on the floor and get some fur therapy or slowly sip a glass of ice water. Having a range of strategies at the ready is key to making sure you can shift your energy when you need to.

Integration Questions

Complete a personal check-in right now. Check into your energy levels. Where are you? What's contributing to your current state of energy? Feel free to use the deflating rubber ducky scale if it's helpful!

What are the top three energy sources that help you feel refueled and ready to rock?

Energy = capacity for impact. Are you funding your energy to your desired level? If not, why not? If so, how could you improve this investment even more?

Consider how proficient you are at shielding your energy. Are there any particular people, places, or situations where you need to put your shields up more often?

Bold on the Inside

Own Your Energy

Bold on the Inside

Strategy #2:

Lead From Your Values

Values don't do you any good unless you actually live and lead from them. Knowing your values but acting out of alignment with them won't help you show up in the world the way you want.

Being bold on the inside also requires external actions, and your leadership actions must be in sync with your core values. This requires knowing what these values are as well as being able to identify whether or not something aligns with them. When your values are clear, they provide a guardrail and a jumping-off point for decision-making. They orient you when priorities are competing and provide context for approaching difficult situations or challenging conversations.

In Action: Lead From Your Values

Authenticity. Integrity. Impact. These are my top three leadership values when it comes to my business. I'd love to say I completed a highly intensive, introspective all-day workshop to develop these, but they came about partially through my previous work and also through my reflection on which clients I enjoyed serving the most in my first few years of being in business. In earlier careers, these same three words tended to be how others would describe me or my work. They resonated with me, but I didn't give them much conscious thought.

As I built my business, I realized that I deeply enjoyed a lot of my work, but occasionally, there would be something that just didn't feel like a right fit. As I reflected on why that happened, it became obvious that the engagements that didn't feel exactly right were ones where I was being asked to compromise one of those three core values. Clear core values don't just provide explicit guidelines for decision-making and make it easy to identify aligned opportunities, they also make it easy to quickly discern when clients aren't a good fit.

A number of years ago, I was asked to provide a proposal for diversity, equity, and inclusion training for an organization that felt it was ready to make its first foray into this type of work. They weren't outwardly known as a progressive institution, so I was very excited about the opportunity.

I partnered with a co-facilitator who was highly regarded in the space, and we put together a comprehensive proposal. Our contacts at the organization were enthusiastic and positive about our plans, and we set things in motion. Right before we signed the final contracts, however, a member of their team called me. "Nicole, everything looks great except for one thing. You can't use the words diversity, equity, or inclusion."

It's rare for me to find myself without something to say, but this was definitely one of those times. Mystified, I responded, "What are we supposed to call it?" Their answer: "Respect and kindness." I didn't even need to call my co-facilitator to know whether or not we were going to serve this organization. It was so obvious they weren't ready for work that would actually make an impact. I knew I wouldn't be able to show up as my authentic self, and it would have been well outside my integrity to accept a contract, knowing there was such a massive disconnect with the organization I was supposed to serve.

Circumstances won't change your values, but you may need to prioritize different values at different times depending on the situation. I also use this strategy of leading from values to manage my work and life as I integrate and navigate between the two. It eases my decision-making about everything from how I spend my time to what I eat and where my money goes. As you operate from a values-based orientation, you will eventually notice that sometimes your values will compete with one another. In my experience, it's not always possible to lead from every single value in every single situation.

As a small example, I have a very strong family value. I want to be a present and active parent for my daughter and a present and active partner for my spouse. I also highly value alone time as a way to recharge my energy. These two often compete in terms of which one I want to prioritize at a certain time, so I need to be strategic in my choices and make sure they're aligned. If I continually give all of my energy away to my family and don't take the time I need for myself so I can be at my best, that doesn't help me show up as the person I want to be for them. Similarly, if I'm constantly away by myself or holing up in my office or behind the locked bathroom door (admittedly a last retreat for solo-recharging!), I might not be fully living up to my value of how I want to show up for my family.

In the workplace, I've held strong values of inclusion and efficiency. Much of the time, I have been able to integrate those two successfully. I've been able to involve team members or create processes where many voices can be involved and timelines are still met. However, there are occasional circumstances when one value needs to be prioritized over the other for various reasons. Extending or renegotiating a deadline might be more important because it is critical to have a highly inclusive decision-making or production process. Conversely, sometimes, a decision needs to be made under tight time constraints.

Having clarity around your values creates a more straightforward path. It provides affirmation and confidence that you're taking action that aligns with who you are and how you want to show up in the world. Though they may evolve as you have new life experiences, values are long-term and provide deep roots as you navigate and adjust to what life and work throws at you. They're an excellent way to help people understand you and your leadership decisions, and it's also incredibly powerful information to know about those around you.

Practices to Help You Lead From Your Values

1. De-fuzz your definitions.

Not only do you need to know what your values are, but you must have absolute clarity on what you mean when you articulate each one. If I say I have a value of generosity, it requires further definition so I can make sure I'm really living in alignment with it. For me, while financial giving is part of that, I define generosity much more broadly. I want to be generous with my time and energy: I want to make room in my calendar to meet with people and help them out. I want to be generous with my financial resources: I will give to organizations and opportunities I care about that align with my other values, and I will do so at an amount and level that allows me to continue to be generous with my own desires. I also extend generosity to myself: I give myself grace when things don't work out exactly as planned, give myself the support I need to feel and be my best, and am kind to myself.

Having crystal clear definitions prevents you from acting in ways that may seem like you're living your values but actually aren't. If I responded to my value of generosity in the way it's commonly defined—purely as financial support—I could easily be pressured to give beyond my means or feel like I needed to give to every appeal. It could be defined outwardly as generous, but it wouldn't match my personal definition.

2. Know what your values look like when you live them.

Taking the definition a bit further, invest time in understanding what it means for you to live your values and put them into practice. Identify what behaviors are present, what actions you take or don't take, and how you feel when you're living in and by your values. Think about how you treat others and how you treat yourself. Create concrete understandings of what your values look like when you live them so you can align your actions and also recognize when you're out of alignment with how you want to be putting your values into action.

3. **Pick your priorities.**

   Sometimes, we find ourselves in a "yes, and..." situation. We can have multiple values and still be committed to those values, and we also may not be able to prioritize all of them at once. Intentional prioritization of values can prevent indecision or unnecessary and unhelpful self-critique. When you're clear on which values you're prioritizing and why, your action steps follow more easily.

4. **Don't negotiate your values with yourself or others.**

   Prioritizing your values is one thing, but negotiating or disregarding them is something else entirely. If you're going to be bold on the inside, there has to be an equally bold commitment to living fully within your value system. This means they become non-negotiable ways of showing up for yourself and showing up in the world. Regardless of the situation, your values guide your behaviors. It might not be easy, but it will be evident.

Integration Questions

What are five of your top values, and how do you define them in terms of your own distinct leadership approach?

What does it look like in action or what does it feel like when you are living these values?

How have your values helped you make a difficult decision or navigate a challenging situation?

What do you need to remember so you can stay boldly rooted in your values and not negotiate them with yourself or others?

Bold on the Inside

Lead From Your Values

Bold on the Inside

Strategy #3:

Choose Courage Over Confidence

You cannot build confidence until you've actually done the thing you're trying to build confidence in. There's literally no other way to cultivate it.

The awesome news is a lack of confidence doesn't have to mean anything other than you simply haven't done "the thing" yet! It doesn't mean you can't act, it doesn't mean you can't try, and it certainly doesn't mean you're not capable of it.

A lack of confidence, however, *is* an invitation to access courage so you can still move forward. Courage is what provides you with the jumping-off place for action. It's not dependent on experience or outcome or anything other than your own personal readiness and willingness to try something in spite of not knowing exactly what might happen.

In Action: Choose Courage Over Confidence

This concept first clicked for me when I listened to the audiobook version of *10x is Easier Than 2x* by Dan Sullivan and Dr. Benjamin Hardy. One specific quote by Dan Sullivan, Co-Founder of Strategic Coach®, totally blew my mind:

"What's the difference between courage and confidence? Confidence feels good."

In one of his articles[1], he explains it even further, "Courage is often depicted as a person feeling absolutely certain about taking action in a situation. That's not courage — that's confidence. The difference between courage and confidence is that *confidence feels good;* courage is doing what you're supposed to do despite the discomfort and the lack of confidence." There's no other way to build confidence than by doing what we want to feel confident about! However, I know that I and a whole lot of my clients have gotten hung up waiting and wanting to feel more confident before taking action. It's a fast way to prevent forward momentum.

What I found so transformative about this idea wasn't so much the basic concept but that it provides clarity for shifting your strategies and what you put into action. You don't have to wait to feel fully confident before taking action or making a decision. Heck, you don't need to have any confidence at all regarding what you're about to do. But you do need to be courageous! Notice the distinction there, too. *You don't have to feel courageous, but you need to act courageously.*

A lack of confidence doesn't have to be a barrier to action. Certainty is not a prerequisite for movement. You must be willing to choose courage in order to achieve your goals, address issues, and take action. This requires an openness to sacrificing the

---

[1] https://resources.strategiccoach.com/the-multiplier-mindset-blog/courage-the-key-to-confidence

comfort of confidence and choosing the courage needed to move forward.

When I was contemplating leaving my longtime local government career and starting a business while having a four-month-old baby at home, you better believe I was praying to feel a massive amount of confidence that would propel me into my desired next steps. I wanted signs, affirmation, and a bones-deep knowing that I could be confident in my success. Too bad that never came! It sure would have made that decision easier. Instead, I finally had to rely on my courage to help me make the move into entrepreneurship. I did all the planning and strategizing and spread-sheeting I could do. There was no other way to get certainty and gain confidence than to make the leap and give it a shot.

I had to come up with a plan to garner the courage to make my move. By nature, I'm a pretty risk-averse person, so the thought of trading my regular paycheck, healthy pension contributions, and schedule predictability was terrifying. I needed to run my numbers and identify financial resources I could access if I needed. I created the top three scenarios in which I would decide to bow out of the entrepreneur game and go back to the safety of my former field. I produced a menu of "deal breaker" situations and circumstances that I wouldn't put my family or myself into so I could recognize them easily and take action if they occurred. I also put together lists of people who were advocates for me and would be willing to help. I wanted a game plan of how I thought I might tackle the first year of being out on my own as a first-time business owner.

Eventually, I exhausted all of those to-do items and was at the point where it was time to make a choice. While I didn't feel an overwhelming sense of calm and ease and still felt like I was about to pull an Eminem and vomit mom's spaghetti on my own Converse, it felt right. I'd done as much due diligence as possible, and it was time to make the leap. I chose courage over confidence and haven't looked back since.

Practices to Help You Choose Courage Over Confidence

1. Distinguish and differentiate.

If you're going to get courageous, you must be able to delineate what you're dealing with. This means knowing the difference between worries and concerns and differentiating between fear and doubt. My friend MacKenna helped me clarify the difference between worries (they have no productive action associated with them) and concerns (they do have productive action associated with them), and it's been a powerful tool for me since.

The same goes for understanding whether you're dealing with fear or doubt because they each have different strategies. Fear is often healthy and makes you consider, "I don't know if I *should* do this." This places you in a position of choice. Doubt, on the other hand, makes you wonder, "I don't know if I *can* do this." Doubt often functions to hold us back and prevents not just forward momentum but even decision-making in the first place. Fear propels us into intentional decision-making. When you know the difference of what you're dealing with, you're better equipped to make your best choice.

2. Decide who you're listening to.

As you live and lead more boldly, there will be plenty of people who have things to say about it. Some of these will be mentors, some will be people in your extended circles of work or family, and there will be no shortage of other humans out and about in the media who are doing their darnedest to tell you exactly what they think you need to know and do. It's your job to filter through the noise and decide what's helpful in terms of your own decision-making.

When I was still an up-and-comer in my first career field (you know, when you're still eligible for things like the "30 under 30" lists), I had a mentor who assured me he had my best interests at heart, and not just in terms of my career but from an entire life perspective. I gravitated toward him because of his extensive experience and background, and he told me he was committed to my success.

One of the things I shared with him early in our mentor/mentee relationship was that I wanted to be successful in my career and I also wanted to have a life. He brushed past this somewhat quickly, assuring me that my life would follow suit as I continued my career growth. Within about a year and a half of our connection, I got engaged. My mentor had known about my long-term dating relationship since my now-husband and I had been opting for what we jokingly called the "five-year plan" of dating before we decided to get married. We'd been dating the entire time I was being mentored, and during a catch-up call, I shared with my mentor the good news that I was finally ready to take the plunge and get married.

My enthusiasm was met with a potent silence. Just as I was about to check our connection, I heard him utter, "You're ruining your career." I was totally shocked. I sputtered a few responses, finally blurting out, "What do you mean?!" He meant exactly what he said. He felt that by getting married, especially to someone who had a pre-teen daughter at the time, I was ruining my career. He was more than happy to provide me with specifics, too. He talked about how I wouldn't be able to move because I was geographically tied to the region now, how I would have to turn down potential dream jobs because I wasn't free enough to say yes to them, how I wouldn't be free to work hundreds of hours because I might have family obligations, and how I would regret this in the long run because I wouldn't be able to have the career he wanted for me. I kept the rest of the phone call short because he clearly wanted no part of my opinion on the matter. (You know, no opinion of my own about *my* life and career.) This was one of many lessons I learned about the importance of having women mentors. I decided I wanted to listen to people who looked and thought a lot more like me.

It wasn't too long after that I decided he was no longer the mentor for me. Taking what he had to say with a grain of salt wasn't going to be enough for me. Heck, an entire shaker of salt wouldn't have been enough. He had outlived his usefulness in terms of my growth and development, and it was time for me to find someone who was more aligned with how I wanted to live and lead. I opted not to have a professional breakup discussion and instead let the connection slowly run its course over time. No doubt that to him, it was further proof that I was frittering away my potential career success by allowing all these silly distractions of love, family, and motherhood. For me? I wasn't worried about it because I was crystal clear that I was listening to myself and doing what was right for me.

I'm not saying this dude never popped into my mind or caused me to question my decisions. That still happened, and even after I got married, I would hear his voice in my head on occasion. The difference was that every time he popped in there, I very quickly decided not to listen to him. Whether you have to do that with an unwelcome voice in your head one time or a million times, it's worth it.

3. Create a habit of courage.

Courage is a habit, not a trait. It's not that you either have courage or you don't. It's a choice, and it's a skill you can practice and strengthen over time. One of my best suggestions for implementing this practice is to stop waiting for it to feel good. Feeling good isn't a prerequisite for something to be good. (It sure is nice when it happens, though!)

Every time you notice you feel hesitant, shy, or a bit unsure about something that either absolutely needs to happen or you simply want to happen, see if you can acknowledge and then release your desire for it to feel good. Then try taking action without waiting for it to feel better. Pay attention to what happens in your body and to your energy before, during, and after you do whatever it is. Over time, you'll build up important data points regarding your courageous actions. Even small steps and actions can create immense momentum toward building your courage habit!

4. **Fool around and find out.**

   Yes, this is commonly referenced with a slightly different f-word at the beginning, but for our purposes here, "fool" will suffice. As you practice choosing courage over confidence, this is an excellent strategy to help you play with it instead of feeling like you need to strap on your research hat and dive into it academically. Test the waters. Play. Have fun with it. Give yourself grace. Lighten it up. Try new things, new responses, or new approaches purely for experimental purposes to see what you can learn. You'll get more comfortable with not needing to have everything figured out, and you'll learn a lot about yourself along the way.

5. **Trust that you are your own best authority.**

   Trust is a conscious choice. This may be a belief you have to live your way into. Over time, as you continue to place trust in your own wisdom, you will gather data that shows it was well-placed. You'll learn to tap into how your body reacts when you're facing a choice. It never lies! The clenching of your tummy, the tightening in your shoulders, or the relaxed opening of your chest—your body always has information for you with clues about how you're really feeling. As you check in with yourself and start to listen for that tiny inspiration from your intuition, you'll notice that you know more about how you want to proceed than you might have realized. You'll make decisions and then evaluate them, creating more of those data points that show the true story of how you've done. Even if you gather data to the contrary and find you need to make different choices, you'll continue to build the practice of trusting your own authority. You won't need other people to help you make decisions, though you may consciously choose to get input from them. You'll know you are enough, and that inner compass will become more and more effective.

Integration Questions

Where have you been waiting to feel more confidence before taking action or making a move?

What is an area of your work or life where you might benefit from choosing courage over confidence?

Thinking of a time when you were courageous in making a decision where you may not have felt fully confident, what did you learn from that experience?

If you were more courageous or felt more confident, how would it impact your leadership approach or impact you could have?

Choose Courage Over Confidence

Bold on the Inside

Strategy #4:

Internalize the Golden Rule

We're all familiar with the golden rule: treat others the way you want to be treated. I love that, AND I also know that many of us have gotten very good at treating others in a caring way while internally being incredibly self-critical or even harmful and downright disrespectful to ourselves.

Instead of feeling like we need to choose one way of applying the golden rule over the other, how about we do both? Treat yourself the way you want others to treat you. This falls into one of those "says easy, does hard" categories for most of us. We have high standards for ourselves and set ambitious goals. Whether somebody else encouraged us to do it or we've developed them for ourselves, our internal expectations can be sky-high. This isn't a bad thing...until it is.

Honest self-review and internal reflection can seriously bolster growth. At the same time, having an inner voice that sounds like an angry, overly-critical drill sergeant with an inferiority complex and turns into negative and berating self-talk instead of positive encouragement to do better will set us back much faster than it could ever take us forward. The same goes for treating ourselves without respect, pushing ourselves too hard, not allowing ourselves to rest, and all the other destructive behaviors we would never direct toward anyone else but seem to allow when it comes to ourselves.

In Action: Internalize the Golden Rule

I hate being rushed. My husband and I had to devise a packing system for when we're going on trips, mainly because it takes me forever to finish packing everything just exactly right. He's generally happy throwing a few shirts, shorts, one pair of shoes, and a stick of deodorant in a grocery bag and figuring out the rest as we go. I, on the other hand, consider every possible contingency and approach packing with the precision of an astronaut preparing to be launched into space for a solo expedition for 9 months without access to additional resources.

In an effort to be helpful, my husband would often come by and zip up my suitcase and take it out to the car, only to hear me screeching ten minutes later, "Where's the suitcase?! I wasn't done with that!" He had no intention (or at least so he says) of trying to rush me or move me along before I was ready, but the fact is, it always makes me feel rushed when he did this or even simply asked, "Are you ready for me to close the suitcase?" We finally had to strike a deal where he would leave me to my neuroticisms, and I would initiate the conversation when I was finally done packing everything the way I preferred.

When I used to work in a more traditional, corporate-type environment, I dreaded the "drop everything and do this now" projects. I'm much more flexible and adaptable now, but back then, nothing threw me off-center faster than one of those types of issues. I enjoyed the thrill of troubleshooting on the fly but hated when there wasn't enough time to research something as thoroughly as I wanted or to engage with as many people as I would typically prefer. I never liked rushing a decision when I felt it could benefit from more time and consideration.

However, if someone were to review what my calendar normally looked like for a long time, you would see nothing but evidence of someone constantly rushing from one thing to the next without enough time for easeful or calm transitions. Sure, there were lots of demands for my time in different ways throughout my career, but I have been a hardcore professional overscheduler since high school. I'd agree to join just one more committee even though I knew I was already overloaded. I'd say yes to in-person meetings requiring travel when I knew it would make things much easier if we conducted business over the phone or in a virtual meeting. I'd squeeze in a phone call (or two!) in that magical 30-minute buffer between meetings. I'd promise myself I would take the afternoon off and then schedule two more last-minute meetings during the time I was going to use to recharge. I'd stay ten extra minutes beyond my desired departure time to finish up "just a few more emails" and then find myself stressing out in rush hour traffic. If I truly don't love this feeling—and I don't—then why on earth was I constantly treating myself this way?

I can't always control all aspects of my schedule and time commitments, but for the most part, if I internalize my own golden rule, I can avoid creating situations where I'm forced to be rushed. This requires some major behavioral shifts. I have to be bold enough to say no when there is a request for my time that requires me to rush or force things into a schedule that I was hoping to keep a bit more open. My internal actions and decisions have to orient not to a place of self-sacrifice and "Well, what other choice do I have?" but instead to outward behaviors that will result in not feeling rushed all the time.

I had to make some serious changes, and I have. I stopped taking meetings before 9:00 a.m. and don't take in-person or virtual meetings on Mondays unless there are serious exceptions due to extenuating circumstances. On out-of-town facilitations, I don't travel the same night I facilitate or speak if it will put me home after 10:00 p.m. I wake up an hour before my partner and my child typically wake up in the morning. For engagements, I don't say yes or agree to any commitments during the first phone call—I make myself review my schedule without the pressure of being on the phone or in a meeting with someone and then get back to them with my decision. I don't take more than three executive coaching meetings in a day. I don't schedule meetings past 3:30 p.m.

None of these were easy changes. Simple, yes, but not easy. They have all required major discipline on my part to set and hold boundaries. They also required a lot of experimentation! I had to find out what felt good and also learn what didn't work. Sometimes, I gave myself way too much space, and the unused time felt worse than being in a time crunch. The bottom line is that if you want your life to feel or operate in a certain way, you have to be willing to treat yourself the way you would want others to treat you.

Practices to Help You Internalize the Golden Rule

1. Figure out your frustrations.

Do you know what a rumble strip is? It's that part of the road outside the white line, where grooves are dug into the roadway. It's designed so that if you're getting too close to the shoulder of the road, the vibration and noise of the rumble strip will alert you as the driver and remind you to get back into your desired space in the lane. I find that frustrations work the same way for me. They are excellent indicators that I'm getting a bit off-track and need to consider a course-correction.

One of my emotional rumble strips is irritation. When practically everything is irritating or frustrating me, it's a clear signal for me to pause and reflect on what's going on. Examine the areas causing you the most frustration or friction to figure out where you could be treating yourself better. Once you've identified them, see how much of that is, in fact, caused by actions (or lack of action) on your part. You'll find great clues about what changes can be made in how you're treating yourself.

2. Become your own best detective.

In addition to figuring out where you could treat yourself better, you'll also need to experiment! Try new strategies or adopt new mindsets, and act like your own detective about it to evaluate what's working and what still needs to be changed. You may not get it right the first few times you try new things, but as you gather evidence of what's working and what's helping, over time you'll be able to refine your approaches.

3. **Emulate and replicate.**

It can be hard to know where to start when it comes to treating ourselves better, so sometimes, it's helpful to look around and find someone to mimic. Who do you have or who have you had in your life that loved or treated you really well? If no one comes to mind, look around at other people or even fictional characters, and you might be able to think of those who are great at caring for others.

Identify a few key actions or approaches you could emulate or replicate. For instance, my coaches are excellent at holding extremely non-judgmental space for me and asking me open-ended questions. My inner voice tends to be wickedly judgmental and overly harsh, and the questions are more like indictments than invitations to explore. I may not naturally be able to do it myself yet, but I can borrow from my coaches' way of doing things and intentionally offer myself a reprieve from judgment. I can also think of a few questions I might ask one of my clients and spend some time journaling on those instead of getting bogged down in the mire of negativity created by my inner critic. You don't have to already be able to do everything for yourself— borrow from some of those best practices around you!

Integration Questions

Which points of friction or frustration from the last month or so could you have controlled for, or where could you have made different choices that might have led to better outcomes for yourself?

Identify some areas in your life where you treat yourself the way you want others to treat you. What helps make it possible in these situations?

Thinking of someone in your life who has treated you really well or someone you have seen, read about, or experienced who has treated others really well, what lessons could you learn to help you treat yourself better?

What are the three smallest things you can do to begin to treat yourself better and more like how you want others to treat you? Get micro. The small changes will add up!

Bold on the Inside

Internalize the Golden Rule

Bold on the Inside

Strategy #5:

Incorporate the Three Empathies

Empathy, meaning the ability to understand or the action of understanding, being aware of, being sensitive to, and vicariously experiencing the feelings, thoughts, and experiences of another, can be an incredible tool in your leadership toolbox. If there was a foam finger that read "Empathy is #1!" you can bet I'd be running around waving it like crazy. Big fan. 10/10 recommend.

I believe there are three distinct empathies that leaders need to take into account and incorporate to lead boldly: empathy for others, empathy for the organization, and empathy for themselves.

Empathy for others is probably the most commonly understood level of empathy. We're familiar with it from principles like servant leadership all the way through religious, family, or school systems, which have taught us to consider others and how our actions might impact them. One of the trip hazards with this kind of empathy is that it's sometimes confused with being unable to hold people accountable. *Empathy and accountability are not mutually exclusive.*

Simply having empathy for someone or a situation doesn't

mean we have to be overly responsive to our new understanding of them or even change our opinions or thought processes. Heck, it doesn't mean that we have to take any action at all simply because we are able to experience empathy for someone else. That being said, empathy is often a precursor to action. It's the thing that helps us understand how we might be able to respond differently to someone else or a challenging situation. Unfortunately, empathy has gotten a bad reputation over time, especially regarding leadership. There is a weird fear I hear leaders share that if they're too empathetic with their team members, they'll be pushovers or perceived as weak. On the flip side, some of them share they have so much empathy for team members that it makes it difficult to hold them accountable.

I love it when leaders are highly empathetic. This creates fertile ground for highly adaptive leadership responses and ways to create cultures that functionally support not just the needs of team members but the needs of the customers they serve. I also love it when leaders have high accountability within their operations. This ensures the work is getting done, progress is being made, and team members are held to productive standards regarding what the operation needs. Both can exist. You can have empathy for your team members, and you can still value accountability and hold others—and yourself—accountable.

The second empathy, empathy for the organization, is the one I believe counterbalances and integrates with empathy for others. When taken fully into account, this is the lens of empathy that keeps leaders from becoming pushovers or allowing bad behavior to persist. They know that if they are also to have empathy for the organization, they can't let poor performance or inappropriate behavior continue. The action they are driven to take considers empathy for the individual and what is important for the organization.

After empathy for others and empathy for the organization, the third is empathy for oneself. When incorporated alongside the other two empathies, this practice ensures leaders are also taking care of themselves while balancing the needs of others and the needs of the organization. Maintaining empathy for oneself helps leaders prevent burnout and self-sacrifice while ensuring they're also not overly orienting to their ego or pride.

In Action: Incorporate the Three Empathies

It was such a relief when I discovered the three empathies and started blending them into my leadership approach! Early in my career, I was often considered a peacemaker or a smoother-over when feathers were ruffled. I had strong communication skills, and I was oftentimes asked to talk with a team member to calm them down or get them on board.

I developed a reputation as the go-to person to send in to speak with angry clients or frustrated teams. It wasn't until I began to practice the integration of empathy for others, empathy for the organization, and empathy for myself in-depth that I got good at it, though. I'd frequently find myself over-identifying with the person who was upset, and my innate sense of justice would set me at cross purposes with what the organization needed from me.

Vice versa was true, too. I could easily see why organizational leaders were making certain decisions, and it frustrated me to no end that some team members refused to acknowledge the difficulty of certain situations and the need for specific actions. Balancing these two helped me communicate differently, and often, it helped me come up with recommendations that merged the needs of both sides of the situation.

It still often left me exhausted. I describe myself as a whole-hearted person who gives 100% and puts my all into what I do. In these situations, though, that math didn't work in my favor because I constantly toggled back and forth between wanting to be 100% on the side of the organization while also wanting to be 100% on the side of the team member or client. That's where I had to learn to have empathy for myself. I had to do a lot of work to learn my limits and draw sharper distinctions around responsibilities and what genuinely belonged to me vs. what wasn't even my obligation to own.

As I coached a participant in one of my women's leadership development programs, she shared a situation where she was struggling. An employee on her team had been going through some difficult personal circumstances—illness, family members who needed care, and mental health issues. The employee needed flexibility in terms of schedule and was often out of work, coming in late, or leaving early. Her performance and work output had diminished, and when she was at work, there were occasions of tears or disengagement from regular team dynamics. As the participant shared her response, she articulated clearly her desire to operate with the utmost empathy for her team member. She was understanding, accommodating schedule changes as much as possible, shifting work around, and even taking on some of her employee's work to lighten the load for them.

I asked how it might look if she considered the situation through the lens of empathy for the organization in addition to empathy for her employee. (Important note—it's not one OR the other—it's both!) In reflection, she shared she had put a lot of time and energy into this one employee in an effort to be kind and supportive, and also acknowledged that some of that was negatively impacting other team members who were picking up additional workload and had to work extra hours to keep up productivity levels. Some of her top performers had begun to grumble a bit about the differences in expectations, and she further reflected that the situation had escalated to the point where she was being impacted in fulfilling her own duties. She realized she wasn't able to do her best to be what the organization needed.

In light of that realization, we explored what it might look like for her to also have empathy for herself. She shared feeling pressured to handle the situation and to keep it from escalating so the organization wasn't impacted. She also felt deeply compassionate toward her employee, who was experiencing so much difficulty and so many challenges. As she considered self-empathy, she also admitted being exhausted and frustrated at picking up extra work and trying to do all the problem-solving.

Since empathy—and particularly when we're balancing the three empathies—leads to action, I asked how she might do things differently when taking into account all three empathies. She decided it was time to set some different boundaries and expectations with her employee, and was sure she could do it in a supportive manner. She committed to talking to the other team members about what had been happening so they knew she recognized the impact on them and also so she could reiterate that she would be supportive of them if they ever faced a similar situation and in case they ever encountered their own set of extenuating circumstances.

She also gained specific clarity that she could no longer

continue to take on so much extra work. Either deadlines and deliverables would need to be renegotiated or else find a way to get her team members to pick up the slack without negatively impacting their existing workloads. She was tired, frustrated, and overwhelmingly compassionate toward all of her team members – and now to herself as well – and was ready to approach it differently.

Practices to Help You Incorporate the Three Empathies

1. **Remember that empathy and accountability are not mutually exclusive.**

   Balance leading with empathy with holding others accountable. Whether you have a situation immediately at hand where this can be utilized or need to study an outside situation and identify how you might respond if you were immersed in it, identify or create responses that value empathy as much as accountability. You might be surprised by what you discover!

2. **Play all sides.**

   When facing a situation, put yourself in the shoes of the other person(s) involved, trying to understand what it might feel like to be them. What are they feeling, experiencing, worried about, or unsure of? What do they need? What do they believe is best for them? What do you believe might be best for them?

   Then, do the same for the organization, asking and answering all those questions. Lastly, do the same for yourself, taking stock of your own experiences and what someone else might believe is best for you or how you would advise a friend in the same situation.

3. **Take yourself (theoretically) out of the equation.**

   Play outsider to your own experiences. If you were an uninvolved, objective third party coming in to examine the situation, what would you observe in terms of each area of empathy? How would you view the others? What would you think about the organization? What would be your thoughts in terms of your role?

4. **Repeat the phrase, "Strong boundaries, strong empathy! Strong boundaries, strong empathy!"**

   Repeat these with gusto! Channel your inner protest marcher for this so you can both inspire and reminder youself. Strong boundaries and strong empathy can both exist together. Do this for yourself so you can do it for others and your organization. You can remain aware of but not be wholly driven by the other person or the circumstances. You matter, too.

Integration Questions

Think of a challenging situation you recently experienced. What empathies were present in how you responded to it? How could your impact have been different if you incorporated all three empathies?

What did you do, or what did they do that made it particularly successful?

What is an experience where you did *not* incorporate all three empathies, and what did you learn from it?

Think of a situation you're experiencing where one area of empathy is out of balance. What would possibly change in this situation if all three empathies were balanced?

Incorporate the Three Empathies

Bold on the Inside

Strategy #6:

Treat Yourself Better Than Your Cell Phone

Our cell phones are an integral part of daily life, practically attached to our hands from the moment we wake up until we go to bed. We put them inside cases, protect their screens, and charge them, regularly bringing them all the way back up to full battery levels. We know how important they are to our daily functioning and treat them accordingly. When the battery level gets exceedingly low, but we aren't able to charge our devices, we'll sometimes put them in battery saver mode, modifying how the phone operates so its battery isn't draining quite as fast to ensure we extend its life as long as possible.

At what percentage of battery level do you start looking for a charger for your cell phone? I'm pretty cautious, so it's about 50-60% for me. I start worrying it won't have the necessary charge later when I need it. I hate not being able to use my cell when I want to, especially when I'm traveling. Entertainment, work, navigation—it's critical! I monitor that darn battery level and make sure I have a portable charging power bank with me in case I can't find a traditional outlet. Even if it's not in danger of fully running out, I'll plug it in and give it some juice if I get the chance. I take care of my phone's battery level because I know how important my phone is.

Why don't we do the same for ourselves? If I asked you what your personal battery level is right now, what would it be? What level have you been consistently operating at for the last week, month, year, or decade? Sure, it fluctuates, but is there a percentage range you commonly find yourself in? Many of us don't consistently recharge our proverbial batteries back to 100%. We might do it once in a while, or we might have practices that bring us back up to maybe 75%, but often, investing the time and attention to getting ourselves fully recharged gets swept by the wayside.

Another common practice I find with my coaching clients (and one I experienced for many years and still struggle with occasionally) is taking time off to recharge but instead using it to get caught up on home or personal to-do lists. Ever blocked a day off to get all your appointments taken care of, take the car for an oil change, get caught up on laundry, and organize and clean out the garage? Battery saver mode. Late night at work with a full day the following day, so you leave work an hour early the next day? I'm glad you're getting some extra time off, but that's likely battery saver mode. What are you doing to intentionally restore your energy?

Treating yourself better than your cell phone is all about managing your personal energy reserves as well as, or even better than, how you treat your device. It honors the importance of running with a full battery when possible or at least consciously paying attention to when your personal battery levels are being drained. You use battery saver mode when necessary, but don't operate that way for extended periods of time. It can be challenging to figure out what actually increases your battery levels, but it's worth exploring!

In Action: Treat Yourself Better Than Your Cell Phone

Full disclosure: I haven't figured this one out all the way yet. I've definitely made some serious strides in this area, but I still have some ups and downs. The boundaries I've put in place around work and how I spend my time have been massively helpful. I've always joked that I don't have an "off" switch, so intentionally creating space where I could integrate rejuvenating practices had to be my starting point. What I fill that time with is critical. As I've gotten older and life circumstances have changed, I've found practices that used to refuel me simply don't have the same effect now. I needed different, more potent methods to get my energy levels back up. I also required way more rest than I've ever required. I had to find alternative sources of support to assist me.

In April of 2023, I was at a low point physically, mentally, and emotionally. I was experiencing significant pain in my lower back and right hip. So much so that I'd stopped working out with my trainer at the gym because it was too painful. I began an intense regimen with a chiropractor and physical therapist and received weekly pain management injections up and down my back to try and calm down my system. One day after I had just finished a session and walked to my car, I recognized nothing had relieved my pain that day.

I sat in the parking lot and bawled because I still had to pick up my daughter from preschool, get her fed, and then hand her off to my husband because I had a four-hour drive across the state to speak at a conference the next morning. I felt panicky because the pain had been so intense over the preceding days that my whole system was overreacting. I could barely eat anything without it completely upsetting my stomach and causing frequent runs to the bathroom, and I couldn't fathom how I was going to be able to drive by myself across the Arizona desert. I knew I was at an inflection point, but didn't know what else to do.

I somehow miraculously made it to the location and gave not just an awesome opening keynote speech but an additional workshop, too. It wasn't without impact, however. My emotional state was beyond agitated, and shortly after this experience, I started on an anti-anxiety medication as well. I met with my chiropractor and physical therapist and told them through my tears I didn't think things were working. They assured me it was a long process and I needed to stick to the regimen. I ignored my intuition, which told me this wasn't helping, and I kept going. My battery continued to deplete.

Six months later, I couldn't do it anymore. I'd only made minimal progress and felt more drained than ever. My body was slightly better, but we weren't making the progress I wanted and deserved after the time and money I'd invested. My energy levels were drained, I was tired and crabby all the time and I started to feel hopeless. I realized that I needed to try something else. Enter Dr. Aubree Bennett.

I did an internet search for a naturopath near me, and that's when I found Dr. Aubree. After reading her website and learning about how she approaches wellness, integrating naturopathic medicine and pranic healing, a type of energy-healing work, I booked an exploratory call. I immediately knew I wanted to work with her. In one session, my pain decreased by 50%, and stayed there. By the end of session two, my pain was gone by about 80%, and stayed away. I was finally on the road to recovery, and as I write this just shy of a year after that first appointment, I'm pain-free and able to address other health issues that have also been draining my battery.

You've got to get plugged into the right places that will restore your energy. You've got to find practices that boost you and sources of support that will help you get refueled. It took a lot of experimentation for me to find this particular one because my old ways weren't giving me what I needed. This isn't just for major health issues causing significant disruption in your life! It's about managing the daily drain of energy or the slow-burning stressors, steadily sapping your strength and well-being over time.

I incorporate other ways of getting recharged, too—I receive regular coaching, joined an entrepreneur development program, take more time off now than I have before, and get together with friends regularly as opposed to letting our visits drift for months (or years!) at a time.

Most importantly, I'm more aware of my energy than I've ever been in the past, and when I notice my battery levels are low or I'm going into battery-saver mode, I don't just keep pushing through. I make sure to get myself plugged back in so my levels can return to where they need to be.

Practices to Help You Treat Yourself Better Than Your Cell Phone

1. **Find what charges you.**

   This is the starting point. What brings back your life and revitalizes your energy? If you already know, right on! If you aren't quite sure, here's the fun part: you get to figure it out. Consciously experiment and see what provides the boost you need. I recommend starting with small practices like journaling, painting, playing with clay, or just going for a mindful walk. Notice what feels good and brings back a bit of life. Go bigger from there—what does it feel like to take an entire hour for lunch away from your desk and your phone? What about a half day off with only fun things planned? A full day? A week? Consider how your downtime is spent and see what's merely letting you veg out and what's restoring your energy.

2. **Get help.**

   There's no gold medal here for only utilizing solo, self-help endeavors to recharge. I say the more, the merrier: hire a coach or join a group coaching circle, engage healthcare or wellness providers for support and relaxation, phone a friend, and get them in on the fun. If you live with other humans or pets, engage them as well. Make some improvements to your home or workspace so it feels more functional and supportive. If you're absolutely stuck and don't know what to do, ask a friend to join in trying new experiences and practices until you figure it out. The journey to identifying your recharge practices can be every bit as fun as actively engaging in them!

3. Do it on the daily.

Fergie did it with the Black Eyed Peas, and so can you. (If you don't know that reference, it's from a highly inspirational song called "My Humps." No judging—sometimes that ends up on my personal recharge playlist!) Engage in daily restoration practices. Think small here. A minute of breathing with extended, slow exhales. A group text with friends who make you laugh. Five minutes of stretching. Sipping on your favorite flavor of fizzy water. Burning your favorite candle. The key to these gestures is the intention behind them and noticing when you use them. Small power-ups can go a long way.

4. Use battery saver mode sparingly.

I've got no problem with battery saver mode as long as there's a full recharge on the horizon. The challenge is that too many of us have gotten accustomed to operating in personal battery saver mode, and it has become the norm rather than something we only use in a pinch. Keep an eye on your battery level, and when that little red warning bar pops up, finish what you need to get through. Then intentionally put your recharge time on the schedule. We need more of what you have to offer this world, so we need you fully charged and ready to go!

5. Don't wait until your battery is low.

You don't always wait until your phone is completely dead before you plug it in. (Okay, some of you might, but you know what I mean!) Recharging and refueling your personal battery levels is a preventative practice, not just something you do when you're so drained that you're barely functioning. Prioritize your own charge levels, and don't let them get so dangerously low that it takes a major recharge session to bring you back to 100%.

Integration Questions

How is your leadership approach different when you are completely recharged and fully fueled?

What drains you at work? At home? In your social circles?

What are the practices that bring your battery levels back to a full charge so you can amplify your impact?

How can you more regularly incorporate recharging practices into your life?

Bold on the Inside

Treat Yourself Better Than Your Cell Phone

Bold on the Inside

Strategy #7:

Be Willing to be Willing

Will·ing·ness /ˈwiliNGnəs/

Noun : the quality or state of being prepared to do something; readiness. "the ability and willingness of workers to migrate"

If you are willing to be willing, it means you are consciously choosing to be not only open to but active in making choices. When leading boldly, this often means being willing to be different, to be talked about, to be uncomfortable, or to be vulnerable.

I think of this as having a vocation of volition. I'm not only capable of choosing for myself, I'm willing to do so and to put that choice into action. Being willing to be willing doesn't mean you have to like what's happening, enjoy the process, or even agree with where you're headed right at the beginning, but it does mean that those things don't preclude you from action. You're not waiting for something to happen; you're happening to something. It's an intentional and powerful place to start so you can make meaningful changes for yourself and move closer to achieving your goals.

In Action: Be Willing to be Willing

Anxiety will often tell me I can't do what I want to do. It won't necessarily feel like something I want to do or even can do, but when I'm willing to do it in spite of the anxiety, I'm always amazed at what I experience. This requires an inherent belief in your ability to pivot. I'll often remind myself that "future Nicole" will figure it out. The more that I've come to trust her (my future self), the more I'm able to try new things and have new experiences.

When I published my second book, *Hot Tub Mommy: Do All Moms Swear This Much?* I wasn't sure what it had to do with my business. I knew I wanted to write it, and it was an important personal journey. While I felt it was connected to my business in some ways, I wasn't exactly certain how it all tied in. It was a totally different type of book than what I'd written before, and I wasn't sure how it would be received. I mean, there are swear words in it—quite a few of them! Generally, I prefer taking action when there's a firm plan or a solid idea of how things might proceed. In this case, it felt like I had no idea where things might go or how it would turn out. I had to be willing to release it without any guarantee or even a strong idea about what this book might mean for me as a person and for my business.

I'd love to say I released it and suddenly the New York Times bestseller list was knocking on my front door, but that's not what happened. It was very well-received and got an incredibly warm reception, but it proceeded totally differently than my other book launch. The conversations have been more personal and intimate, and a completely different audience is resonating with it. I have had to remind myself to be willing to see what this specific experience needs and is evolving to be rather than constantly trying to approach it the way I've done before. To my delight, this process is fun in an entirely different way, and I'm curious to see where it leads!

Practices to Help You Be Willing to be Willing

1. Willingness is a choice.

You consciously have to choose willingness. You can't wait for it to feel good because that may never happen. When I find myself in the space of wanting to be willing but not quite feeling it inside, I remind myself as many times as needed that I'm continuing to choose to be willing. There's no more meaning to my feelings (after all, they aren't facts!) than simply the experience of having them, so I choose willingness over and over again, as many times as it takes. This might be a minute-to-minute thing, or it may just take a few reminders. Regardless, I repeatedly make the conscious choice to be willing, and I act in this way in spite of my reluctance or internal resistance.

2. No pushing allowed.

Being willing to be willing is different than forcing yourself to do something that's genuinely not aligned for you or is an unhealthy decision. I always experience this more as a gentle coaxing or strong encouragement as opposed to forcing. There's a distinct difference between courageous choices and self-abuse. In the same vein, you need to differentiate between conscious deliberation and delay or procrastination. I want you to make well-informed decisions you've thought through. However, if you find yourself intentionally procrastinating rather than making progress, it might be time to look a bit deeper. Check in with yourself to make sure you're aware of these differences and act accordingly.

3. Embrace the "yet."

I was working with a group of students at Arizona State University, and we were discussing their worries and concerns about the coming year of grad school. One student shared that he was very worried about speaking in front of others because he wasn't a good public speaker. "Yet," I added as he concluded his sentence. "You aren't a good speaker *yet*. But if you're willing to do it, you'll get more comfortable over time and build your skill set." You don't need to already be at your own finish line, but you do need to be willing to get there.

4. Don't allow yourself to stay stagnant.

Have well-defined ways to motivate yourself to action. These will look different for everyone. Nike's slogan isn't "Just do it as long as you really feel like it and are 100% certain everything will work out." Sometimes, you've got to get yourself moving and "Just do it." Find out what compels you to take action. For some, it's getting clear on why they want to do something. For others, myself included, it's conquering or overcoming something or gaining mastery of a new skill or experience.

You might have some other reason or practice that helps you become willing to move from stagnation. I set internal deadlines, and when I'm feeling especially stuck, I'll ask others to help remind me or check on me so I can ensure I'm moving forward. When I've got to get myself in gear and get on with something, I'll often clap three times, shake my hands out, and take a deep breath to signal my body and my brain that it's go-time. (If you're a fan of the movie *Gone in Sixty Seconds*, it's nowhere as cool looking as what Nicolas Cage does, but it works for me!)

I also fully embrace the daily to-do list, using calendar reminders and a plethora of sticky notes strategically placed around my office, kitchen, and bathroom mirror. Figure out what works for you. The most important thing is to find strategies that spur you out of stagnation, no matter what they are.

5. Know thyself.

Socrates was a pretty smart dude, and this little phrase, "Know thyself," contains some solid advice. Make sure you know your "unwilling behaviors" as much as your willing behaviors. Recognize when you're simply procrastinating, avoiding, or even lying to yourself and telling stories rather than operating from reality.

I can always tell when I'm avoiding willingness because household tasks that are otherwise unappealing suddenly seem to be of critical importance. I also over-emphasize what others need (or at least my perception of what they need) rather than what I desire. I spin into a thousand what-if scenarios, each more gruesome and horrific than the last. I become hyper-focused on justifying or defending my current position rather than dreaming about what I want. I realize that when these thoughts or behaviors crop up, I need to look a bit deeper and question some of the conclusions I'm coming to. I don't judge myself harshly for these behaviors, but I do recognize them and consider them an invitation to examine my actions so I can possibly choose another course of action.

Integration Questions

What was a time or experience when you decided to "be willing to be willing," regardless of how you might have felt about the situation?

What did you learn from deciding to be willing?

Define your "unwilling" behaviors. What do you do (or not do) when you want something but aren't willing to go for it or explore it further?

If you were more "willing to be willing" about something in your life or career, what would or might become possible for you?

Bold on the Inside

Be Willing to be Willing

Bold on the Inside

Strategy #8:

Operate Independently

This is another one that falls into the "says easy, does hard" category. It sounds easy on the surface, but it can be challenging to put into practice. Operating independently doesn't mean you're alone all the time, although there will be times that's true. It means that you're able to self-sustain when needed, and your leadership isn't wholly dependent on something or someone else. Outside forces don't dictate your actions. They may be in response to them, but they are independently chosen and enacted with purpose.

While you may be operating inside of a larger system, you maintain your sense of self and sovereignty, even when operating within its guidelines. It's about cultivating an internal assuredness that allows you to keep moving forward, even when everyone else is assuming you'll stay stagnant. You're aware of trends and even opportunities, but your forward movement is your own. It might only be happening inside for the time being, but you're able to clearly distinguish your internal compass and direction from any outside influences.

In Action: Operate Independently

My 5-year-old strutted confidently down the hallway, proudly wearing her gold-and-rainbow-cheetah-print unitard with hot pink Crocs on her feet. It was going to be a gorgeous spring day, and she was ready to tackle one more kindergarten adventure. I had gotten this fancy little get-up for her gymnastics class. While gymnastics was no longer a thing, her undying love for this outfit remained. I wasn't quite sure about her wearing it to school, though, so I did a quick check-in with her, "Are you sure you want to wear that and maybe not something that's more comfortable and easy to get in and out of when you need to go to the bathroom?"

Looking at me like I was the dumbest person in the world, she responded by simply sliding it down off her shoulders and around her ankles to demonstrate how easily she could access the bathroom when the time came. As she hauled the straps back up over her tiny shoulders, I asked, "Does it feel good when you wear it?" to which I received an enthusiastic, "Oh yeah, Mommy. I love it!" The outfit of the day was decided.

That afternoon, when I picked her up and we walked to the car, she grabbed my hand and looked up at me. "Mom, some of the kids made fun of my outfit today." A dagger straight to this Mom's heart, of course, so I squeezed her hand and looked her straight in the eyes while contemplating appropriate ways to make kindergarten-age tormentors suffer. "I'm sorry that happened. But what do YOU think of your outfit? Do you love it? I know I love it on you!" My little girl didn't even miss a beat, "Yeah, I do. It's pretty awesome." We decided popsicles were clearly the next best step after a day like that, so off we went.

Operate Independently

Operating independently doesn't mean everyone else jumps on your gold and rainbow cheetah print unitard train. In fact, it almost ensures that people won't be sitting in your same cheering section. Instead, this practice is about you charting your own course and feeling the inner courage to be able to continue to do so. It's knowing that your particular path to leading boldly doesn't have to—and probably won't—look like anyone else's or even anyone else's idea of what it should look like. And that's not just okay; it's pretty awesome. And powerful.

Practices to Help You Operate Independently

1. No outside input required.

Ask and answer these two power questions relentlessly: Do you like it? Does it work for you? Make sure you're giving an honest answer to both! These are integral to my self-sustenance practices. When there's a solid yes to both, I'm much more energized to approach whatever situation I'm facing. No outside input required.

2. Give yourself credit.

Give credit where credit is due, and that includes YOU. Own your awesomeness here—it might be your flashy outfit or your willingness to adventure far outside of your family's expectations. Even if it's simply making it through a meeting without letting that snarky comment past your lips or your inner feelings show on your face, you deserve some credit. When you're operating independently, it can be easy to slip into a space of feeling like you're not making progress or that no one will ever understand or accept you.

While both of those are potentially possible, neither of them are likely. Operating independently means there may not be an audience full of raving fans at your disposal to recognize your efforts and provide appropriate support and appreciation. You're going to have to do that for yourself, and it starts with honestly giving yourself credit for everything you're doing.

3. Decide your own definitions.

There are a lot of people willing to provide you with their definitions of how you should operate and what your success or even self-worth should look like or feel like. You need to decide your own definitions. What does success look like? What does it mean to feel you have self-worth? What does "working hard" mean for you? What does a day well-spent look and feel like in your experience? Make sure you write up a broad list here. I often find I need to write a new definition for myself when I'm getting frustrated with outside expectations or when someone says something (even if it's well-meaning), and it sort of rankles and gets under my skin. Only you can decide what your definitions mean.

4. Pen your own permission slips.

We grow up needing permission from others. In school, we need passes to go to the bathroom or a permission slip to go on a field trip. We ask parents or guardians for permission to see our friends, borrow the car, or dye our hair hot pink. Rules often exist for reasons, but we literally grow up normalizing the need for an outside voice to give us permission before taking action on what we want to do. Self-governance and independent operation means you don't have to wait for someone else to tell you something is a good idea, or that you're ready, or even that they think you should do something. You pen your own permission slips when you need them. In actual practice, I will sometimes sit down and write myself a permission slip as a visual reminder—it's helpful to see it in writing, and I love seeing my own signature on there!

5. Stop the storytelling.

In communication, we tell stories and apply meaning all the time. We observe someone do or say something, and usually, without checking with them, we instantly tell a story about them. Arms crossed? Couldn't possibly be cold, they're definitely closed off and don't like what I'm doing. Eye roll? Can't be something in their contact, they're rolling their eyes at me and being disrespectful. Cut me off in traffic? No way they might just have diarrhea, they're definitely just an a-hole with no sense of regard for human life. If you're going to operate independently, you've got to manage the stories that you tell about the humans and situations around you. Ask yourself these four questions to help you manage the stories you're telling:

- Did you tell yourself a story without facts or with perceptions?
- What meaning are you adding to the action you observed?

Bold on the Inside

- Why would a reasonable or rational person say or do this?
- What is your role in the conflict?

Integration Questions

Write about a time when you operated independently. What did it feel like? What did you consider in your course of action? What did you learn?

What is your definition of success?

Think of somewhere you might be letting someone else define what you should be doing or how you should be doing it. What would you like to change about this so you can be more distinctly YOU as a leader?

What support would you need, or what would need to change in order for you to operate with more independence?

Bold on the Inside

Operate Independently

Bold on the Inside

Strategy #9:

Establish a Support Squad

Support squads aren't just groups of people who make you feel good, although that's one important function of them. Whether they are an actual group or a collection of individuals, they provide literal support to you when you need it. You might meet or be in contact with them regularly, or you may interact with them more sporadically. You could get together with them socially, or it may be more formal and professional. Your support squad members might know you on a very personal level, or they may be contacts and connections who only know certain aspects about who you are. Regardless of who is in your support squad, you can be sure that when the time comes, they're there for you and they'll be willing to help you out. Your support squad always has your back.

In Action: Establish a Support Squad

I've always excelled at being there for other people. Like, basically expert-level support squad member for lots of other people. You need me? I'm there wearing a t-shirt with a picture of your face on it and waving a foam finger with your name and "She's #1!" on it. On the flip side, I wasn't always good at cultivating an intentional support squad for myself. I was social and had an active life, doing things with friends and interacting with many people on the professional side, but I confused being outgoing and having social interactions with cultivating my support squad.

In recent years, however, I've learned just how vital my support squad members are for my own well-being as well as for my career growth and professional advancement. As my career progressed while working in local government, I intentionally built and deepened relationships with mentors who took the time to get to know me and who were willing to make time for me when I needed them. It wasn't a huge number of folks, but I specifically asked them if they would help me grow, and they always showed up for me. I made sure that I didn't interact with them only when there was a request or a problem but that we also connected when things were going well. They invested their time in me, and I honored that investment.

I also have a support squad in a business entrepreneur coaching group led by my coach, Natalie Miller. I meet with Natalie 1:1 once a month, and weekly she creates a space for myself and some other amazing entrepreneurs where we come together to build skill sets, hold space for each other, learn, self-reflect, and grow. Not only is Natalie someone I consider integral to my support squad, but because she has built a space where I can connect with other entrepreneurs, I count these other folks as part of my support squad, too. Often, one of us says, "It's so great to hear someone else is experiencing this. I felt so alone..." and immediately thereafter, we are met not just with support but with insight and reflective questions to help us grow in the area we want to improve.

My brunch bunch shows up a bit differently! Almost every month, a group of five of us get together for brunch. It's a fun, social atmosphere with lots of laughs and plenty of carbs to go around. As we've regularly met over the last few years, our friendships and connections have deepened, and while the conversation isn't always something that has great depth or potential meaning and impact for the universe, it matters to us. I know I can count on that bright spot, and the ensuing text message chains that result from our conversations often bring a little bit of unexpected joy to my days and leave me smiling and feeling more energized. They've offered help unasked for, celebrated with me, commiserated with me, and held non-judgmental space for me to share ideas and explore.

Some of my boldest moves, both on the inside and the outside, have come because I knew I had a support squad to help me and be there for me when I was ready to rejoice over a victory or console me after something didn't go the way I hoped. Support squads are more than just cheerleaders who are excited for you; they do meaningful work and invest their time and energy in your success.

Practices to Help You Establish a Support Squad

1. Find your folks.

In order to have a support squad, you've got to have people to fill those slots. This might be online communities or connections you've made through professional websites and trainings, or it can be humans in the flesh you can sit down across a table from and share a cup of coffee with. Some of my most influential support squad members are people I've never even met outside of a virtual meeting setting!

You can find them through professional organizations, connections of colleagues, your current workplace, hobby or interest-based groups, volunteer opportunities, or even previous places you've worked. You can't be shy when establishing your support squad—this is the time to be bold on the outside as well as bold on the inside. Make the ask, offer the invitation, and coordinate the get-togethers. It's worth it.

2. Diversify your membership.

The best support squads have a diverse range of members who are all there for various purposes. Think about it as having different people on your list for different reasons. Some members will provide encouragement and give you that pep talk when you need it; some are highly experienced in the areas where you want to grow and can provide both mentoring and advising; some help you blow off steam and relax; and some might be able to help you remember who you are. I say the wider the range, the better!

3. Connect with intention.

Connections with your support squad members can be ad hoc, but be intentional when you're interacting with them. Think through what you need from the connection and how you want to ask for their support. It may be an overt request, or it could be something more subtle, like simply wanting to have fun and escape the to-do list or the worry list for a while. For some types of support, regular interactions or connection points might be a better idea than trying to schedule something on the fly. Do what works for you, and do it intentionally.

4. Show up for your support squad members, too.

Make sure you're showing up for your members in return. After all, these are the people providing the right kind of support and connections for you to live a life that's truly bold on the inside. How can you support them right back? What do they need from you? Get that foam finger ready!

5. Express your gratitude and appreciation.

Regardless of why someone is in your support squad or how they ended up there in the first place, it's important to express your gratitude and appreciation for them being there. Of course, this just feels good, but it's also a way of saying, "Hey, you're making a difference, and I hope you stick around for more!" As you get to know them better, you can offer it in ways that are more meaningful for them. I like to think of this as a small way of helping them get more of their magic out in the world, too.

Integration Questions

Who do you already have on your support squad, and who might you want to add?

Where in your life do you want more support?

What would be possible for you if you felt truly supported?

How can you show appreciation to some of the members of your support squad in the next month?

Establish a Support Squad

Bold on the Inside

Strategy #10:

Stop Shoulding Yourself

Shoulding yourself is that thing we do when our inner voice begins to rail at us about all the other things we *should* be doing or choosing besides whatever it is we're actually doing or choosing. There's an entire chapter on this in my first book, *Awesome on Your Own Terms: Intentional Practices to Help You Stop Shoulding and Start Succeeding*. Heck, it even made its way into the title! Other people can "should" all over us, too. It's exhausting.

Part of being bold on the inside is learning to control that inner monologue and what gets spoken between your own two ears. You may not be able to stop the initial "should" from some of your internalized messages but you can choose what to do with it. Someone else may do it to you intentionally or even inadvertently, or you might read or see something that flips this trigger for you. When we stop the shoulds, it's a way of stepping back into direct control of what we're doing. Actions that follow will be more aligned, and you'll know you're the one fully in charge of what you're doing.

In Action: Stop Shoulding Yourself

I am notoriously hard on myself. I often refer to this as much as a shadow as it is also a superpower. Everything from how I'm spending my time, whether or not I went and worked out, how messy my house is, you name it, I'm pretty good at "shoulding" myself over it. It's a fast track to guilt for sure, and it doesn't usually lead me anywhere that's very productive. When I decided to launch my business and leave my former career, the shoulds were stronger than I had ever experienced. *You're almost to the top! You should stay a little longer! So many people need you, you should continue to stay and serve them. Local government is a noble profession, you should stay in a career that has direct service. You should stick with something stable and proven that has a good retirement, not risk it all trying to start your own business!*

Those words came from my own brain as much as they came from anyone else, and they totally muddied the waters. It was hard to hear my true inner voice when all of these statements were crowding it out. I finally got fed up one day and shared them all with my partner. He listened intently and kept asking me what else was in there—what else was I saying to myself or what else I was hearing. After I finally dumped it all out there for him to see and sift through, he reminded me that I was shoulding all over myself and so were these people.

I couldn't stop other people from saying what they were going to say, but I could choose to act in spite of their input. First, however, I needed to stop further complicating an already complicated situation by continuing to should all over myself. We agreed that I would be more vocal in expressing what was going on in my head so I could more clearly sort it out. That brought immense relief, and in what felt like no time at all, I was handing in my resignation and launching my new adventure.

This always makes me think of something I once heard Elizabeth Gilbert say when I saw her in person on her book tour. A woman behind me asked a question about a friend of hers who was struggling to support her daughter. The daughter felt she had made a huge mistake by having an intimate relationship with a boy she was seeing. Her decisions had gone against the advice of her family and her church. As many teenage romances go, it hadn't worked out, and now the girl was feeling horrible about herself, regretting and questioning her decision. Liz spoke with such love when she shared that what she would say to her would be, "Oh, honey. How could you possibly have done anything else?" She went on to explain that this version of shoulding ourselves comes from blaming previous versions of ourselves (who don't have our same experiences and insight) for making certain decisions when it would have been virtually impossible to have done anything other than make that same decision. How could we have? We didn't know!

Practices to Help You Stop Shoulding Yourself

1. Filter frequently.

For this strategy, "filter" should become your new favorite f-word. You're going to have a lot of different voices in your head, including your own voice, telling you what you should or shouldn't be doing. Again, just because you might hear them doesn't mean you need to listen to them. Consider what's going on in that internal chatter or what is coming in from the outside, and filter accordingly. Once you've filtered out what's unhelpful or feels like a should, check one more time and filter again.

2. Keep perspective & forgive yourself as needed.

I find I have to zoom out regularly to maintain perspective when the shoulds start to take over. It's important to adjust your perspective in order to have a clear way to evaluate what the shoulds are saying. And remember, honey, how could you have done anything differently? You literally didn't know what it would be like. Go easy on yourself and practice self-forgiveness. Even—and maybe especially—if you're worried you don't deserve forgiveness or peace, try offering it to yourself instead.

3. Engage an ally.

Sometimes, it's hard to get out of this cycle all by ourselves. If it's feeling especially sticky or you've noticed an excessive habit of shoulding yourself or letting someone else should all over you, try asking someone to help you keep an eye on it. My husband does this for me, as do most of my friends and even my clients!

4. Cultivate awareness of your inner self-talk.

Write down what goes through your head. Say it out loud, even if it makes you cringe. When it remains only as something that's happening in our head, it's too easy for us to minimize it. When you force yourself to express it in writing or say it verbally to another human being (or even your cat), you'll hear it differently. This helps you work on that perspective and also provides an opportunity for some much-needed questioning of your thoughts.

5. Be clear on your own desires.

When I'm reminded that, deep down, I don't even want to be backpacking through Nepal, or climbing Kilimanjaro, or owning the giant house with five bathrooms, or driving the latest Tesla, it provides a strong measure of relief and allows me to refocus. It's so easy to get caught up in wanting things that other people want or want for you that you can lose sight of what's specifically right for you. When we're bold on the inside, we want what we want without needing approval or affirmation from anyone but ourselves.

Integration Questions

When in your life has someone else "should" all over you, or when have you done that to yourself?

Is there anywhere in your life currently where you are still "shoulding" yourself?

Instead of "shoulding" all over yourself, what would you rather tell yourself instead? If it makes it easier, pretend you're talking to a friend. What would you want them to hear?

What is something that could help you maintain a healthy perspective and stay away from the "shoulds" when they happen?

Stop Shoulding Yourself

Bold on the Inside

Strategy #11:

Practice Professional Pit Stops

Over the last five years or so, I've become a fan of Formula 1 car racing, which has led to other unexpected forays into auto racing. Thanks to my partner, I eventually bumped into the 24 Hours of Le Mans race, an endurance-focused sports car race held near the town of Le Mans, France. Unlike most races, which are fixed-distance, the 24 Hours of Le Mans race is won by the car that covers the greatest distance in 24 hours. Teams must balance all sorts of factors, including speed, driver fatigue, the car's ability to run without mechanical failure, maintenance on the vehicle throughout the race, and race strategy. They utilize pit stops to assess performance, provide fuel, repair what needs repairing, and adjust strategy in order to get a better outcome.

As I work with coaching clients, organizations, and teams of all sizes across industries throughout the United States and Canada, this is a fitting metaphor. There's some very pertinent wisdom to be found. What caught my attention the most was the intentional effort spent to identify a pit stop strategy that supported the most optimal outcome for the team. This means creating intentional, dedicated, and repeated focused time to refuel, assess resources and maintenance needs, reconsider strategy, and redirect/recommit to a plan of action. This helps ensure optimal performance for the longest amount of time to achieve the greatest amount of progress.

Your pit stop strategy is unique to your journey. This might be a regular cadence of time set aside to identify the most critical activities, refuel or recharge, set intentions for the future, and evaluate ongoing performance. You will do this your own special way, and remember—the most important part of a professional pit stop is that it happens at regular intervals, so you can keep showing up as your best!

In Action: Practice Professional Pit Stops

I incorporate a variety of pit stops. There's a quick pit stop before I pick up my daughter from school to make sure I'm ready to transition to the energy afternoons require. I briefly evaluate what was accomplished, identify plans for that evening or the next morning, do a quick pick-up of my office, and grab a snack and one more glass of water before going to get her. This usually only takes a few minutes, but it helps close out the work day and allows me to shift into a different gear for family time.

Quarterly, I have a check-in call with one of my coaches. We review commitments from previous calls and assess progress, troubleshoot current challenges or issues, talk about what I'm doing to keep myself and my business sustained, and set goals for the upcoming quarter. I leave feeling excited about what I've accomplished and with a distinct plan on how I'm moving forward.

Annually, I do a pit stop right around the start of the new year.

Practice Professional Pit Stops

Sometimes, it falls on New Year's Day, but usually, it's during the last week of December. I'll take a few hours with my journal to reflect on the year, eat something yummy, celebrate my progress, identify lessons learned, and come up with my word or phrase for the new year. I love taking the time to exhale, relax, and celebrate while also keeping an eye on the future and what I'm hoping it brings. Selecting my word or phrase feels like outlining my strategy for the coming year, and I get excited about what's possible!

Occasionally, we'll do a pit stop as a family. We had one of these recently, and it was lovely and refreshing for all of us. I'd been noticing that everyone's stress levels were rising, and we all sort of seemed to be out of gas energetically. Tempers were flashing hotter than normal, and it felt like we'd been pushing at a frenetic pace for a long time without much downtime to rejuvenate. It had started to feel like every evening was turning into the potential for a 3-person cage fight with each of us giving serious side-eye, trash-talking, and waiting for someone to make the first move so we could jump all over them.

We went to a cabin in the mountains for a long weekend, and we agreed that rest and relaxation were the most critical things on our to-do list for the weekend. Then we agreed to basically throw the to-do list out altogether. On the drive up there, my partner and I caught up with each other in an unhurried way. It felt luxurious to have three and a half hours of doing nothing but talking if we felt like it. We didn't end up doing much planning or strategizing over the course of the weekend, but we rested. Deeply. Coming home and getting ready for the week felt calm and happy instead of frantic and rushed.

Practices to Help You Practice Professional Pit Stops

1. Create a cadence.

It's important to have a plan for the frequency of your pit stops. Professional racing teams usually have several options outlined for their pit stop strategies so they can respond to what happens during a race. I like to have a planned cadence of when I'll take pit stops so I know when I have those points in my schedule to take time out for a bit. You might play with a daily, weekly, monthly, quarterly, and even annual pit stop schedule. See what feels best, but make sure you're trying them out regularly enough to gather evidence of what's working!

2. Plan your pit stops.

I love a good agenda like Cookie Monster loves cookies, especially when it comes time for a professional pit stop. Identify the core things you want to accomplish, include time for refueling and recharging your energy, define the purpose of the pit stop, assess performance and take stock of accomplishments, evaluate what's working and what needs a tune-up, and then set your strategy for what happens post-pit stop.

3. Put together a pit crew.

In racing, pit stops are a team endeavor. Engage others around you to help you plan or execute your pit stop. Try incorporating someone to help you optimize the utility of your pit stop. Maybe you need help with something, some assistance in reflecting on progress or setting new goals.

Practice Professional Pit Stops

Maybe you need someone to help you recharge, or maybe you need someone to take something off your plate so you are able to disconnect. Having a pit crew will help you make the most out of the time you set aside.

Integration Questions

When have you taken a professional pit stop to rest, refuel, evaluate your strategy and projections, repair things that need repair, or change directions? What was your biggest takeaway from the experience? (If you've never done this yourself, do you know someone who has? What can you learn from their experience?)

What did this strategy make you think of in terms of how you are approaching your professional trajectory?

What would your ideal pit stop look like on a daily basis? Weekly? Monthly? Quarterly?

Who do you need in your pit crew, and what do you need them to do so you can have a more effective, useful, and professional pit stop when you do take one?

Practice Professional Pit Stops

Bold on the Inside

Strategy #12:

Change Yourself First

B old leaders first create change within themselves so they can create it elsewhere. It's virtually impossible to change something externally if you haven't changed it internally yet. Want more peace? Gotta be more peaceful. Need more spaciousness in that schedule? Time to stop overcommitting, overdoing, and overscheduling. Desiring more kindness and respect around you? Make sure you're treating yourself that way. Change can be hard, but it doesn't have to be. When we work on internal changes first, it helps us develop a blueprint for making changes externally.

In Action: Change Yourself First

It was 2015, and I was sitting in the audience at the International City and County Management Association conference. Pat Martel, an amazing leader I'm now privileged to know, was the incoming president, and as she shared her remarks, she also issued a call to action. The organization had just released its task force report on women in the profession, plainly showing there had been little to no progress made toward equity between men and women leaders in the local government profession over the preceding 30 years.

Pat challenged all of us to do something about it. She reminded us that the power to make the change we all wanted to see was already within and up to all of us sitting there listening to her speak. It stuck with me, and even though I wasn't entirely clear on what was possible or what I might do, I knew I would do something.

Fast forward a few months later when I was talking with a friend who was also a leader in the local government space. I shared the experience with her, and we decided to formalize a group that had been informally operating in our state. The official version of Arizona Women Leading Government was born!

We decided to kick things off by putting together a half-day meet-up, inviting women leaders we knew from across the state. We thought it would be amazing if we could get 50 to 70 people to attend. To our surprise and delight, we had to cut off registration at 225 attendees because we had maxed out the occupancy level for the ballroom we had rented for the day. Pat Martel came and spoke at that gathering, and I've always remembered how impactful it was to see the outcome of the change we both hoped to inspire. Transforming myself into an active leader who supports women in advancing their careers in local government helped me see what was possible when we make changes in ourselves to pave the way for the larger changes we aspire to achieve.

I've taken that lesson with me, especially when working with my coaching clients. So many of my executive coaching clients come to me to work on issues of busyness and overwhelm. They feel hopeless, out of control, and like there's no possible solution or hope for it ever feeling any different. For a long time, I felt stuck because I honestly empathized with them and hadn't solved those problems for myself yet!

I wondered if it was even something I should be talking to clients about. I didn't have any answers for them, and although coaching is about asking great questions rather than providing answers, I felt so mired in sharing the same experience that it made it difficult for me to stay objective in the sessions. I sincerely committed to making changes in this area and quickly realized all of us were right. It was dang hard to start to make shifts! External forces, old habits, actual pressures of family and social systems... all of it has an impact. However, as I began to unwind my own addiction to being busy and loosening some of the strangleholds my productivity addiction and overwhelm had created, I was able to see things in a new light. As I developed new tools for myself, I also discovered and invented new ways to help my coaching clients. When we change ourselves first, we make changes for others possible, too.

Practices to Help You Change Yourself First

1. Knock off your own nonsense.

Get real with yourself. Look within and identify ways you self-sabotage or let yourself get distracted from making the internal changes you want to see. Take note, and then take action. As you become aware of how you take yourself off track, you have an easily-identifiable list of behaviors and actions to avoid now.

2. Shore up support.

Just because it's an internal change doesn't mean you have to do it alone! Share your inner journey with someone who's in your corner, or put it out there online. Once other people know you're working on this, not only can they keep you accountable, but they can help support you in changing.

3. Monitor progress.

Every small step counts. If you've ever played a game of telephone, you know how quickly one small change can generate a huge mix-up further down the line. It all adds up. The snowball effect is real, so use it to your advantage. Give yourself the credit you're due and take note of how far you've come, even if it initially feels tiny. Every win you celebrate will motivate you to make more progress.

4. Remember that clarity and focus are your friends.

Make sure your goal is clear. What exactly are you trying to change? Why is it important to you? What do you hope happens once you've changed it? Stay focused, too. Keep your desired change front and center. Write it on sticky notes and place them everywhere—your car, your bathroom mirror, your monitor, even the inside of the toilet lid if you think that will help. Create a recurring self-check-in on your calendar to remind you what you're trying to achieve and see how you're doing. Ask a friend to text you once a week to ask how things are going. Holding a strict focus will help ensure you maintain momentum and keep moving forward.

Integration Questions

Where do you see the need for change in your life, at work, in your circles, or in society?

Where do you see echoes of these needed changes in your own life or behaviors?

What do you most want to change about yourself first so that you can more positively impact some of these other changes?

What becomes possible for yourself and for others when you make your desired changes?

Bold on the Inside

Change Yourself First

Bold on the Inside

Strategy #13:

Understand and Own Your Influence

Understanding and owning your influence is a core strategy for becoming bold on the inside. Unapologetically, you internalize and accept your capabilities, the level of influence you can exert, and what you have to offer. It's not about an ego trip; it's about assessing where you are in relation to what you want to happen. When you understand and own your influence, bold action follows more readily. You know where you stand, who you might be able to help, and how you might be able to help them. Even in cases where you don't desire any external shifts, understanding and owning your influence changes you on the inside.

In Action: Understand and Own Your Influence

I'd just stepped off stage from delivering a morning keynote at a conference for school business leaders across the state of Arizona. A woman I barely knew came up to me and said, "You and I will be following up SOON." Alrighty then! I went about the rest of the day and went home. A few weeks later, I had a meeting with her to talk about establishing a women's executive leadership development program for the organization that had hired me for the keynote. I was floored. My speech hadn't even been aimed at this audience or touched on those topics necessarily, and I'd been feeling under the weather to boot! She didn't know me at all. Who was I to do this?

But wait, who was I to *not* do it? I remembered that I'd already led a program like this for a client in California who was looking for internal support programs for their team members. I thought of the countless women I'd coached and the amazing women who had coached me. I was at a completely different point in my career and business trajectory. I'd gained tools and had experiences that would help me build a program suited specifically for the women they wanted to help. I had a level of influence that exceeded what I'd been recognizing in myself. I was ready to own that and get to work supporting these leaders and helping them grow. As soon as I embraced my own influence, I got excited about what I could offer these women leaders.

Practices to Help You Understand and Own Your Influence

1. Depersonalize it.

Gain objectivity on your own influence by treating yourself like someone you don't know. If you were meeting you (as another human, of course), what would you understand about your experience, your connections, and the knowledge you have gained? What type of influence do you think that would give someone?

2. Complete an honest accounting.

Take stock of what you've done so far. Give your life and professional career a quick review. Go back over your experiences and things you have learned that might position you as an authority. You will likely discover you've learned more than you're giving yourself credit for. Also, take special note of any instances when people have looked to you for help, assistance, or as a model for what to do.

3. Ask someone else.

If it's hard for you to get a better feel for your influence or if you simply want to expand your purview, ask someone you trust who knows you very well. Chances are, hearing it in someone else's words might help you internalize it further and help you see yourself—and your influence—a little differently.

4. Try it on.

I once had a friend express surprise at a newfound level of influence she was experiencing. "Nicole, they were, like, actually asking me my opinion! And then LISTENING to it!" She was doubting her influence in the situation and was having a bit of a hard time owning it, so I suggested she just try it on. "What would it feel like to own that level of influence? What would that change about how you approach your ongoing work?" If you're not ready to totally own it, try renting it for a while and see how that feels.

5. Figure out how far the fulcrum is.

A fulcrum is the point on which a lever rests and on which it pivots. Where the fulcrum is along the lever and where you are in relation to it will dictate how easy or hard it is to get the lever to pivot and move. Consider what you hope to influence. How far from the symbolic fulcrum of the situation are you? What kind of force must be exerted to make change? Will it be easy for you? Will it be incredibly difficult for you? Knowing how far you are from the fulcrum will help you understand exactly how much influence you can have in a situation. This is the clarity you'll need to help you figure out your way forward.

Integration Questions

Think of someone you know who is highly influential. How do they understand and own their influence?

What would your mentor or one of your best friends say about the type and level of influence you have or how you could continue to grow?

When was a time you knew you had influence in a situation? What helped you understand and own that influence?

If you had more influence in an area of your life, how would that help you amplify your impact?

Bold on the Inside

Understand and Own Your Influence

Bold on the Inside

Strategy #14:

Look for Launchpads, Not Cushions

In a coaching session once, I described a particular area of my business as a comfortable cushion. It was a place to rest where I was making a good, dependable income. While this wasn't necessarily a bad thing, what I hoped for at that stage of the evolution of my company was more growth in a specific niche area beyond what this cushion place had to offer. I loved working with women leaders, and I wanted to do more in that space. The issue was having a slate full of clients who wanted other types of work that I had historically offered. As I was talking, I realized that what I needed was a launchpad, not a cushion.

Don't get me wrong, there's nothing wrong with being comfortable. I think that's a great place to be, and I welcome it when I find it. However, if you're looking to be bolder on the inside, you're going to need a launchpad, something that you can use to go forward to something better or more important.

Launchpads might be new approaches you take to solving old problems, cultivating new connections, investing in learning experiences to help you think differently or grow, saying yes to a new position or offer, or any other number of things that propel you forward. It might even be a home meditation practice or a new routine that mixes things up for you. Launchpads are meant to do just that: launch. They spur you to new places, new experiences, and new skill sets. You'll have time to rest on those cushions post-launch!

In Action: Look for Launch Pads, Not Cushions

Early in my local government career, I was asked to step in as the Interim Director of Parks, Recreation, and Libraries. While I grew up using these amenities and was a big fan of the services they provided, I had absolutely zero background in running the operations. I was strong in finance, knew the basics of HR, was proficient in the general machinations of local government processes, and was completely out of my comfort zone when it came to running this department. Heck, at that point, the most supervisory responsibility I'd ever had came from an unpaid intern I'd been the point of contact for!

I'm a team player at heart, and I knew I wanted to support my colleagues as well as make my boss happy. Turning down such a significant opportunity wasn't a course of action I was willing to consider, but I was distinctly uncomfortable at the thought of taking on such a huge responsibility. I finally realized I wasn't just getting out of my comfort zone; I was stepping onto a launchpad that would shape the trajectory of my career. And I was right!

I handled problems I'd never even known existed, set up systems and procedures that were missing, dealt with some unequivocally wild personnel situations that would have made more seasoned managers cringe, and was absolutely humbled by my own learning curve.

I also learned the correct way to reset portable toilets that have been knocked over when you show up to the 4th of July event the night after a monsoon storm has come through. (Hint-make sure you set them back up from the side that does not have the door, or you'll be wearing all that lovely blue liquid and getting it in your mouth and squishing through your shoes. Lesson learned the hard way. Thank goodness they hadn't been used yet!)

That experience as Interim Director radically accelerated the growth of my skill sets and provided adventures that directly led to later promotions. More importantly, it launched me into a completely new stratosphere in terms of my understanding of how to work with people. It wasn't smooth sailing by any means, but it was massively important in helping me learn lessons I desperately needed to integrate.

Practices to Help You Look For Launch Pads, Not Cushions

1. Evaluate the outcomes.

Even if you don't know exactly where a decision might lead, do your best to forecast what might happen. Feel free to put a few alternative scenarios together and play with some different outcomes. Make sure you compare this to staying where you are and see which one feels better. Which route might be the launchpad you need?

2. Figure out how comfortable you really are.

Like I mentioned earlier, there's nothing wrong with being comfortable. Cushions exist for good reason! That being said, however, there's a difference between enjoying a comfortable space and staying stagnant. What kind of comfortable are you?

3. **Check in on your current trajectory.**

Will what you're doing now get you where you want to go? If so, keep on truckin'. If not, what might be worth exploring to give you the launchpad you need? What might move you forward faster? Don't be afraid to ask for help with this one from someone who knows you well or has already gotten to where you want to go.

Integration Questions

What area of your career would you most like to experience growth in?
What specifically would you like to be different?
Based on your current trajectory, are you heading in the direction you want to go?
What do you think is serving as a cushion for you that might be keeping you in place where you're at?
What kind of launchpad do you think would help you most in terms of achieving your goals?

Bold on the Inside

Look for Launchpads, Not Cushions

Bold on the Inside

Strategy #15:

Ideate, Implement, Iterate

I love a good strategic plan. I also love jumping right into the work with minimal planning, executing, and then iterating along the way. As a strategy for becoming bold on the inside, "Ideate, Implement, Iterate" is important because it is consistently action-oriented. Spending a significant amount of time in the strategizing and planning phase of things can be tempting. Ideating is the risk-free space where you get to dream, and it's an essential stage of the process.

With this strategy, you spend a little bit of time there, but the bulk of your effort goes toward implementing the thing you're considering. You give yourself a reasonable amount of time to gather data about what is working and what you'd like to change, and you move quickly to iterating and making adjustments. You tweak things, sometimes throw the whole idea out and start over, and basically uplevel your approach. There's no judgment over what didn't work, simply gratitude for the knowledge gained. You keep your focus on how to continually improve what you are already doing.

In Action: Ideate, Implement, Iterate

About seven months after I launched my business full-time, I was working on my laptop in the evening after our daughter finally fell asleep. My husband looked at me and simply offered an observation without judgment and with compassion, "You know, babe, you don't work any differently now than you did before."

That observation stopped me in my tracks. He knew that one of the reasons I decided to go into business for myself was to gain freedom over my time. I had spent almost a decade and a half working at the mercy of schedules I didn't set for myself. Plenty of night meetings and weekend commitments. A rigidly defined expectation of when I would be at work. Demanding positions where 90% of each work day was spent in meetings, where those overscheduled daytimes led to a survival-based approach with catch-up occurring in the wee hours of the morning, late at night, and over the weekend. I was definitely not fulfilling my desire for why I had started the business.

It was the wake-up call I needed. I'm not saying I never work in the evenings now, get up early to get ahead on things, or take time on the weekends to work. The difference now is that I do those things intentionally. They are the exception and not my rule. Getting to this point has taken a ton of ideation, implementation, and iteration. I have tried what feels like 8,700 different ways to approach my work schedule. I've worked with three different assistants to help me manage my time and build new methods of accomplishing work. I've taken numerous coaching courses and listened to countless webinars, podcasts, and audiobooks. I consistently felt like a failure when a new method didn't work out exactly how I was hoping it would or when the functionality of it waned over time.

Now, when I try something new to manage my work style, I don't try to solve for the entire problem for the entire rest of my life all at once. I come up with something new, start trying it out, evaluate how well it is or isn't working, and then iterate on it. Every evolution has brought me closer to a work life that genuinely feels good!

Practices to Help You Ideate, Implement, Iterate

1. **Remain committed to the process but unattached to the outcome.**

   I first learned of this strategy in therapy. I was in deep grief after losing my beloved mom very unexpectedly, and I remember telling my new therapist that I "just wanted to feel better as quickly as possible." While that was very much true for me at the time, it maybe wasn't the most realistic approach. As an experienced therapist, she recognized this and asked that I commit wholeheartedly to the process while remaining unattached to the outcome. She was very clear that this didn't mean giving up the desire to feel better quickly, but she encouraged me to expand my perspective so I could have the freedom I needed to engage in sessions without worrying about why I wasn't feeling better yet. Commit to the process of ideating, implementing, and iterating, and hold space for things to evolve the way they need to. You'll learn, which means you'll still be well ahead of where you were.

2. **Improve your distress tolerance.**

   Time for another lesson from Nicole's therapy journeys. A different therapist introduced me to the term "distress tolerance," which essentially means a person's ability to manage actual or perceived distress (i.e. you're able to sit longer with that discomfort without it being overly problematic). As he shared the idea with me, it was quickly apparent I had some learning to do in this space. None of us like to be uncomfortable, but we can learn to improve our tolerance for discomfort. Committing to ongoing iteration means you're never quite DONE all the way, which can feel odd or even uncomfortable. Building a higher level of distress tolerance will help you implement this strategy.

3. **Identify the upward spiral.**

   As you integrate and utilize this strategy, it's not uncommon to feel like you're getting stuck in a holding pattern or simply repeating an unhelpful cycle over and over. While these are only stories you're telling (because the reality is you're always moving forward if you're continuously iterating!), they can be distracting and demotivating. Consider your "ideate, implement, iterate" cycles as an upward spiral. You're not staying stuck in one place, and even though the progress might feel minimal, I'll bet you that you're always spiraling upward. As long as you're learning, it's considered a win. Look for where you have built upon previous experiences and let that fuel you to keep trying for more.

Integration Questions

Where do you need to develop an idea and try out a new approach to help you put your own unique style of leadership into action?

Think of a time you tried something and then iterated on the initial idea. How can that experience help you with something you're currently facing?

If you gave yourself permission to implement something quickly and then iterate upon it, what would you be doing that you are not currently doing?

If you accept the idea that you're never completely done and will always be iterating, what freedom does that give you?

Bold on the Inside

Ideate, Implement, Iterate

Bold on the Inside

Strategy #16:

Honor Your Instincts

To me, honoring your instincts means respecting and keeping an internal agreement with yourself to live by your values, respecting your own thoughts and ideas, and acting accordingly. This strategy is all about alignment. It's about slowing down long enough to hear what your intuition is telling you, to feel where your instincts are guiding you, and to be willing to have the courage to act accordingly. Your instincts will always speak, and you need to be willing to listen. A bold leader will not only know what their instincts are telling them, but they will honor them.

This is not about acting on whims and being driven by thoughtless impulses. It requires the willingness and the intentional practice to hear and operate by what your instincts are trying to tell you. You will have choices to make about abiding by your instinct or being led by more conventional wisdom or approaches. Only you will know the difference, but trust me, you will definitely recognize the difference.

In Action: Honor Your Instincts

Your instincts will lead you in minor situations as much as in major ones. Once, while facilitating a particularly challenging group, I decided to address the elephant in the room: nobody wanted to be there, and most were upset at the perceived misuse of a workday during a busy time. To get the participants talking, I asked everyone to share what they would rather be doing than sitting in my facilitation for the day.

One long-tenured team member standing in the back was all too willing to oblige me as he pointed his finger at me while making full eye contact and shared, "I'd rather be deployed than sitting in this room with you." I've been a professional facilitator long enough to have experienced my fair share of venom and frustration, and it poured off of him in waves. I've also been a professional facilitator long enough to have honed some pretty keen instincts.

Prior to getting the day started, I'd introduced myself to each team member individually. I wanted to get to know a bit more about them because I'm genuinely interested in knowing who is in the room. A side benefit I've found is that this practice often reveals useful background knowledge once the courageous conversations start occurring. In this case, I knew that part of his frustration came from the fact that over his multiple decades with this organization, he'd been through at least two other rounds of this type of facilitation to try and solve the same problems they were experiencing. I couldn't blame him one bit; I'd be frustrated, too!

My instincts told me to honor his long-term commitment and experience while also engaging him as part of the solution instead of an opponent. So, without missing a beat when he told me he'd rather be deployed than sitting in the room with me, I responded, "That's a pretty significant comparison. I know you've been through this before, and I'd be frustrated, too, if I were you. I'm glad you have so much experience, because I'd love to start with you when we get going. I have a feeling you can help us get through the conversations faster and maybe get out of here earlier."

It was an action-packed session after that, but by the halfway point on day two, he pulled me aside and said, "You know, Nicole, the problem isn't that we're not talking to each other. We talk all the time. The problem is that we're not listening to each other." Talk about a mic drop moment! He was absolutely right, and I was grateful he had been an active participant throughout the engagement.

Practices to Help You Honor Your Instincts

1. Practice hearing your instincts.

I love my fellow high-achievers, but it can be darn hard for us to hear our own instincts sometimes. We get lost in the to-do list, overly focused on output, or caught up in too much doing to hear what our instincts might be whispering. Learning to hear your instincts can be a trial-and-error practice. Many of us don't pause long enough or give ourselves enough down time to even hear our instincts. A lot of leaders I know have been operating in crisis mode for so long that they've forgotten how to even stop long enough to hear what their instincts are telling them. Experiment with things like journaling, silent walks or workouts, meditation, or even just incorporating more regular personal check-ins to begin to hear your instincts more clearly. Most importantly, before you make a decision or react to something, stop, listen and feel your way into what your instincts might be telling you. Consider whether or not it's at odds with what your brain or other people might be telling you to do.

2. **Explore your instincts.**

   Personally, I love to do this with a partner, but you can do it on your own as well. Use the integration questions below, or craft a few of your own. Ask your instincts to speak loudly and pay attention throughout the day. When you're significantly tuned in to exploring what your instincts have to tell you, they will speak to you all day long. Pause for a moment or two before you take any action, even deciding between the burrito or the burger for lunch. Let your instincts have a say before you do!

3. **Treat your instincts as a beloved advisor.**

   You wouldn't just ignore a mentor or coach who you genuinely trust, right? When you treat your instincts as a beloved advisor trying to give you helpful and supportive advice or direction, it allows you to listen to them in different ways. Honor what they're telling you, and take note of what you learn.

Integration Questions

Thinking of a time you ignored your instincts, what did you learn from the experience?

What have you learned from experiences where you honored your instincts, even if it maybe didn't make as much outward sense at the time?

What might change if you honored your instincts more deeply in particular areas of your life?

What is one practice you could regularly incorporate to help you honor your instincts more?

Bold on the Inside

Honor Your Instincts

Bold on the Inside

Takeaways and Commitments

When I facilitate, I always end my sessions with takeaways and commitments. Each team member identifies at least one takeaway from the experience and makes a commitment to themselves or their team in terms of what they will do differently to integrate the lessons from the session.

Now that you've read and reflected on all 16 strategies, take a moment to think about what you're taking away from this book. What have you learned? What else came up for you while you were reading this, or what did the strategies bring to mind? Your biggest takeaway might be something you actually read, or it could be a conversation that the book prompted or an experience you had while reading it. It doesn't matter what it is; it's more important to reflect and find out what you're taking forward with you. Also, consider how you want to be different now that you've read it. What do you want to commit to start doing or maybe even stop doing?

The prompt questions below will help you hone in on your takeaways and commitments. Use some of the strategies shared throughout the book to help keep you on track toward making the change you want to commit to. No matter what you choose, as long as it feels true for you, you'll be on the road to becoming bolder on the inside.

Reflection Questions

What is a key takeaway (or key takeaways) from reading *Bold on the Inside*?

What else came up for you while reading this book that feels important to remember?

What is one commitment you want to make to yourself regarding how you want "to be" now that you've read this book?

What support will you need to provide yourself or receive from others to keep that commitment?

Takeaways and Commitments

Bold on the Inside

Conclusion

The day after I finished writing the chapters for *Bold on the Inside*, I went for a walk to try and figure out how I wanted to conclude the book. Nothing immediately sprang to mind as the exact right way to wrap it up. I think that's because the work doesn't end once you've finished reading this book. This isn't the kind of work that ever ends! Not only in the sense that you can return to these strategies and the integration questions again and again, but also in the sense that the upward spiral of your leadership journey is never over.

If I had to pick two words to send you forward with, they would be celebration and integration. First, celebrate every single little ding-dong win, all the ways you've shown up as bolder on the inside, and every step forward you take.

Integration is the other word because I mean it in terms of making real shifts in how you approach your work and leadership. Whether it's these 16 strategies or others you encounter or develop along the way, keep integrating and keep growing. Not only will your leadership work become more potent and powerful, but you will set an important example for others, and sometimes the example you set is the most powerful instigator to positive change.

We need you as your own sparkly unicorn self. We need you in your workplace and in your community, leading and living in the ways most aligned with your truest self. We need the unique gifts only you can offer. We need your insights, your intellect, your humor, your quirky individual personality, and the brightness you have to offer. When leaders are bold on the inside, they can create bold changes on the outside. This world feels like it could use some bold changes.

I love the idea of it starting with you.

Appreciations:

Sean Lance, you are my ultimate hype-man and cheerer-on. Thank you for helping me make time for this project and for all of your encouragement, the times you made me laugh, and the ridiculous texts you sent me from the jacuzzi while I was writing this. I love you.

Rochelle Dailey, your wizardry with calendaring and wicked-fast response times any time I have a request is so massively appreciated. Thank you for creating the space to bring this into being!

Justin Fulton, thank you for believing in me and for your excitement about this project. You infused energy into it at a time when I needed it. Thank you for being such a light in the way you lead!

Kevin Evans, early in my career, you taught me one of the most important phrases I've ever learned: "Don't overreact, but don't underreact." Your mentorship shaped me into the bold leader I am now, and I am grateful for you.

Bob Wingenroth, you are one of the boldest, most authentic leaders I've ever encountered. From the first time we met and you asked me what brought me joy to your support and encouragement as I embraced motherhood and, ultimately, a completely new career path, your insightful questions and unwavering confidence in me encouraged me to do more than I ever dreamed possible for myself.

Lenore Cerniglia, ending up as roommates with you freshman year at Arizona State University decades ago feels like fate. You were so completely authentic, self-confident, bold, and completely unintelligible when your Italian New York accent got thick - it was one of the first times in my life I felt completely free to be me, and I'm so glad you were along for the ride.

Lindsay Smith, I've never encountered another human as committed to their personal growth as you. I've watched you live, lead, and love your way through some incredibly daunting situations while remaining unerringly true to who you are. You are the boldest of the bold, my friend.

Natalie Miller, dang, lady, what can I even say? Your coaching and friendship have provided not just the actual tools but the support to help me live my life as boldly as possible and build a business that's as bold as possible. Eternally grateful for what you have helped me discover.

Heather Wilde, your patience with my Voxer challenges (FFS!), encouragement, laughs, and tangible support made this project possible. I grin every time my phone lights up with your name on it, and I am grateful for you and all you are in this world. Thank you for reminding me time is irrelevant, even when I have a timeline, and for helping me to see myself as so much more than I sometimes allow myself to be.

Jennie Jolly, your editing magic is unmatched. Thank you!

Chani Becker, your creativity and artistry brought the cover to life in a way I couldn't have dreamed. So grateful for you.

Liz Amys, Ellen Herman, and Evelyn Youngquist, thank you for shaping this book by being beta readers! Your attention, intention, and insightful feedback truly improved the final version. I'm so grateful for your energy and assistance.

About the Author

Nicole Lance is an entrepreneur, proud mom and stepmom, happy partner to her husband Sean, and ignorer of laundry piles. When she's not cussing over the Lego bricks her daughter leaves scattered on the floor, you can find Nicole journaling and writing in her big, yellow chair, working with coaching clients, facilitating with teams, and speaking at conferences. She is the author of *Awesome on Your Own Terms*, *Hot Tub Mommy*, and *Bold on the Inside*.

Connect with the Author

Nicolelance.co
Facebook.com/NicoleLanceCoaching
LinkedIn.com/in/nicolelance
Instagram.com/nicolelancecoaching

Leave a Review

If you enjoyed reading *Bold on the Inside*, would you consider leaving a review on a platform of your choice? Reviews help indie-published authors find more readers like you.